C-1072 | CAREER EXAMINATION SE

THIS IS YOUR **PASSBOOK®** FOR ...

ACCOUNTING EXECUTIVE

NATIONAL LEARNING CORPORATION®
passbooks.com

COPYRIGHT NOTICE

This book is SOLELY intended for, is sold ONLY to, and its use is RESTRICTED to individual, bona fide applicants or candidates who qualify by virtue of having seriously filed applications for appropriate license, certificate, professional and/or promotional advancement, higher school matriculation, scholarship, or other legitimate requirements of educational and/or governmental authorities.

This book is NOT intended for use, class instruction, tutoring, training, duplication, copying, reprinting, excerption, or adaptation, etc., by:

1) Other publishers
2) Proprietors and/or Instructors of «Coaching» and/or Preparatory Courses
3) Personnel and/or Training Divisions of commercial, industrial, and governmental organizations
4) Schools, colleges, or universities and/or their departments and staffs, including teachers and other personnel
5) Testing Agencies or Bureaus
6) Study groups which seek by the purchase of a single volume to copy and/or duplicate and/or adapt this material for use by the group as a whole without having purchased individual volumes for each of the members of the group
7) Et al.

Such persons would be in violation of appropriate Federal and State statutes.

PROVISION OF LICENSING AGREEMENTS. — Recognized educational, commercial, industrial, and governmental institutions and organizations, and others legitimately engaged in educational pursuits, including training, testing, and measurement activities, may address request for a licensing agreement to the copyright owners, who will determine whether, and under what conditions, including fees and charges, the materials in this book may be used them. In other words, a licensing facility exists for the legitimate use of the material in this book on other than an individual basis. However, it is asseverated and affirmed here that the material in this book CANNOT be used without the receipt of the express permission of such a licensing agreement from the Publishers. Inquiries re licensing should be addressed to the company, attention rights and permissions department.

All rights reserved, including the right of reproduction in whole or in part, in any form or by any means, electronic or mechanical, including photocopying, recording, or by any information storage and retrieval system, without permission in writing from the Publisher.

Copyright © 2022 by

NLC®

National Learning Corporation

212 Michael Drive, Syosset, NY 11791
(516) 921-8888 • www.passbooks.com
E-mail: info@passbooks.com

PUBLISHED IN THE UNITED STATES OF AMERICA

PASSBOOK® SERIES

THE *PASSBOOK® SERIES* has been created to prepare applicants and candidates for the ultimate academic battlefield – the examination room.

At some time in our lives, each and every one of us may be required to take an examination – for validation, matriculation, admission, qualification, registration, certification, or licensure.

Based on the assumption that every applicant or candidate has met the basic formal educational standards, has taken the required number of courses, and read the necessary texts, the *PASSBOOK® SERIES* furnishes the one special preparation which may assure passing with confidence, instead of failing with insecurity. Examination questions – together with answers – are furnished as the basic vehicle for study so that the mysteries of the examination and its compounding difficulties may be eliminated or diminished by a sure method.

This book is meant to help you pass your examination provided that you qualify and are serious in your objective.

The entire field is reviewed through the huge store of content information which is succinctly presented through a provocative and challenging approach – the question-and-answer method.

A climate of success is established by furnishing the correct answers at the end of each test.

You soon learn to recognize types of questions, forms of questions, and patterns of questioning. You may even begin to anticipate expected outcomes.

You perceive that many questions are repeated or adapted so that you can gain acute insights, which may enable you to score many sure points.

You learn how to confront new questions, or types of questions, and to attack them confidently and work out the correct answers.

You note objectives and emphases, and recognize pitfalls and dangers, so that you may make positive educational adjustments.

Moreover, you are kept fully informed in relation to new concepts, methods, practices, and directions in the field.

You discover that you arre actually taking the examination all the time: you are preparing for the examination by "taking" an examination, not by reading extraneous and/or supererogatory textbooks.

In short, this PASSBOOK®, used directedly, should be an important factor in helping you to pass your test.

ACCOUNTING EXECUTIVE

DUTIES

Supervises and directs the accounting and fiscal services in a large institution or department; performs related duties as required.

SUBJECT OF EXAMINATION:

The written test designed to evaluate knowledge, skills and /or abilities in the following areas:

1. General accounting and auditing;
2. Governmental accounting;
3. Administration and supervision;
4. Understanding and interpreting tabular material; and
5. Preparing written material.

HOW TO TAKE A TEST

I. YOU MUST PASS AN EXAMINATION

A. WHAT EVERY CANDIDATE SHOULD KNOW

Examination applicants often ask us for help in preparing for the written test. What can I study in advance? What kinds of questions will be asked? How will the test be given? How will the papers be graded?

As an applicant for a civil service examination, you may be wondering about some of these things. Our purpose here is to suggest effective methods of advance study and to describe civil service examinations.

Your chances for success on this examination can be increased if you know how to prepare. Those "pre-examination jitters" can be reduced if you know what to expect. You can even experience an adventure in good citizenship if you know why civil service exams are given.

B. WHY ARE CIVIL SERVICE EXAMINATIONS GIVEN?

Civil service examinations are important to you in two ways. As a citizen, you want public jobs filled by employees who know how to do their work. As a job seeker, you want a fair chance to compete for that job on an equal footing with other candidates. The best-known means of accomplishing this two-fold goal is the competitive examination.

Exams are widely publicized throughout the nation. They may be administered for jobs in federal, state, city, municipal, town or village governments or agencies.

Any citizen may apply, with some limitations, such as the age or residence of applicants. Your experience and education may be reviewed to see whether you meet the requirements for the particular examination. When these requirements exist, they are reasonable and applied consistently to all applicants. Thus, a competitive examination may cause you some uneasiness now, but it is your privilege and safeguard.

C. HOW ARE CIVIL SERVICE EXAMS DEVELOPED?

Examinations are carefully written by trained technicians who are specialists in the field known as "psychological measurement," in consultation with recognized authorities in the field of work that the test will cover. These experts recommend the subject matter areas or skills to be tested; only those knowledges or skills important to your success on the job are included. The most reliable books and source materials available are used as references. Together, the experts and technicians judge the difficulty level of the questions.

Test technicians know how to phrase questions so that the problem is clearly stated. Their ethics do not permit "trick" or "catch" questions. Questions may have been tried out on sample groups, or subjected to statistical analysis, to determine their usefulness.

Written tests are often used in combination with performance tests, ratings of training and experience, and oral interviews. All of these measures combine to form the best-known means of finding the right person for the right job.

II. HOW TO PASS THE WRITTEN TEST

A. NATURE OF THE EXAMINATION

To prepare intelligently for civil service examinations, you should know how they differ from school examinations you have taken. In school you were assigned certain definite pages to read or subjects to cover. The examination questions were quite detailed and usually emphasized memory. Civil service exams, on the other hand, try to discover your present ability to perform the duties of a position, plus your potentiality to learn these duties. In other words, a civil service exam attempts to predict how successful you will be. Questions cover such a broad area that they cannot be as minute and detailed as school exam questions.

In the public service similar kinds of work, or positions, are grouped together in one "class." This process is known as *position-classification*. All the positions in a class are paid according to the salary range for that class. One class title covers all of these positions, and they are all tested by the same examination.

B. FOUR BASIC STEPS

1) Study the announcement

How, then, can you know what subjects to study? Our best answer is: "Learn as much as possible about the class of positions for which you've applied." The exam will test the knowledge, skills and abilities needed to do the work.

Your most valuable source of information about the position you want is the official exam announcement. This announcement lists the training and experience qualifications. Check these standards and apply only if you come reasonably close to meeting them.

The brief description of the position in the examination announcement offers some clues to the subjects which will be tested. Think about the job itself. Review the duties in your mind. Can you perform them, or are there some in which you are rusty? Fill in the blank spots in your preparation.

Many jurisdictions preview the written test in the exam announcement by including a section called "Knowledge and Abilities Required," "Scope of the Examination," or some similar heading. Here you will find out specifically what fields will be tested.

2) Review your own background

Once you learn in general what the position is all about, and what you need to know to do the work, ask yourself which subjects you already know fairly well and which need improvement. You may wonder whether to concentrate on improving your strong areas or on building some background in your fields of weakness. When the announcement has specified "some knowledge" or "considerable knowledge," or has used adjectives like "beginning principles of…" or "advanced … methods," you can get a clue as to the number and difficulty of questions to be asked in any given field. More questions, and hence broader coverage, would be included for those subjects which are more important in the work. Now weigh your strengths and weaknesses against the job requirements and prepare accordingly.

3) Determine the level of the position

Another way to tell how intensively you should prepare is to understand the level of the job for which you are applying. Is it the entering level? In other words, is this the position in which beginners in a field of work are hired? Or is it an intermediate or advanced level? Sometimes this is indicated by such words as "Junior" or "Senior" in the class title. Other jurisdictions use Roman numerals to designate the level – Clerk I, Clerk II, for example. The word "Supervisor" sometimes appears in the title. If the level is not indicated by the title, check the description of duties. Will you be working under very close supervision, or will you have responsibility for independent decisions in this work?

4) Choose appropriate study materials

Now that you know the subjects to be examined and the relative amount of each subject to be covered, you can choose suitable study materials. For beginning level jobs, or even advanced ones, if you have a pronounced weakness in some aspect of your training, read a modern, standard textbook in that field. Be sure it is up to date and has general coverage. Such books are normally available at your library, and the librarian will be glad to help you locate one. For entry-level positions, questions of appropriate difficulty are chosen – neither highly advanced questions, nor those too simple. Such questions require careful thought but not advanced training.

If the position for which you are applying is technical or advanced, you will read more advanced, specialized material. If you are already familiar with the basic principles of your field, elementary textbooks would waste your time. Concentrate on advanced textbooks and technical periodicals. Think through the concepts and review difficult problems in your field.

These are all general sources. You can get more ideas on your own initiative, following these leads. For example, training manuals and publications of the government agency which employs workers in your field can be useful, particularly for technical and professional positions. A letter or visit to the government department involved may result in more specific study suggestions, and certainly will provide you with a more definite idea of the exact nature of the position you are seeking.

III. KINDS OF TESTS

Tests are used for purposes other than measuring knowledge and ability to perform specified duties. For some positions, it is equally important to test ability to make adjustments to new situations or to profit from training. In others, basic mental abilities not dependent on information are essential. Questions which test these things may not appear as pertinent to the duties of the position as those which test for knowledge and information. Yet they are often highly important parts of a fair examination. For very general questions, it is almost impossible to help you direct your study efforts. What we can do is to point out some of the more common of these general abilities needed in public service positions and describe some typical questions.

1) General information

Broad, general information has been found useful for predicting job success in some kinds of work. This is tested in a variety of ways, from vocabulary lists to questions about current events. Basic background in some field of work, such as sociology or economics, may be sampled in a group of questions. Often these are principles which have become familiar to most persons through exposure rather than through formal training. It is difficult to advise you how to study for these questions; being alert to the world around you is our best suggestion.

2) Verbal ability

An example of an ability needed in many positions is verbal or language ability. Verbal ability is, in brief, the ability to use and understand words. Vocabulary and grammar tests are typical measures of this ability. Reading comprehension or paragraph interpretation questions are common in many kinds of civil service tests. You are given a paragraph of written material and asked to find its central meaning.

3) Numerical ability

Number skills can be tested by the familiar arithmetic problem, by checking paired lists of numbers to see which are alike and which are different, or by interpreting charts and graphs. In the latter test, a graph may be printed in the test booklet which you are asked to use as the basis for answering questions.

4) Observation

A popular test for law-enforcement positions is the observation test. A picture is shown to you for several minutes, then taken away. Questions about the picture test your ability to observe both details and larger elements.

5) Following directions

In many positions in the public service, the employee must be able to carry out written instructions dependably and accurately. You may be given a chart with several columns, each column listing a variety of information. The questions require you to carry out directions involving the information given in the chart.

6) Skills and aptitudes

Performance tests effectively measure some manual skills and aptitudes. When the skill is one in which you are trained, such as typing or shorthand, you can practice. These tests are often very much like those given in business school or high school courses. For many of the other skills and aptitudes, however, no short-time preparation can be made. Skills and abilities natural to you or that you have developed throughout your lifetime are being tested.

Many of the general questions just described provide all the data needed to answer the questions and ask you to use your reasoning ability to find the answers. Your best preparation for these tests, as well as for tests of facts and ideas, is to be at your physical and mental best. You, no doubt, have your own methods of getting into an exam-taking mood and keeping "in shape." The next section lists some ideas on this subject.

IV. KINDS OF QUESTIONS

Only rarely is the "essay" question, which you answer in narrative form, used in civil service tests. Civil service tests are usually of the short-answer type. Full instructions for answering these questions will be given to you at the examination. But in case this is your first experience with short-answer questions and separate answer sheets, here is what you need to know:

1) Multiple-choice Questions

Most popular of the short-answer questions is the "multiple choice" or "best answer" question. It can be used, for example, to test for factual knowledge, ability to solve problems or judgment in meeting situations found at work.

A multiple-choice question is normally one of three types—
- It can begin with an incomplete statement followed by several possible endings. You are to find the one ending which *best* completes the statement, although some of the others may not be entirely wrong.
- It can also be a complete statement in the form of a question which is answered by choosing one of the statements listed.
- It can be in the form of a problem – again you select the best answer.

Here is an example of a multiple-choice question with a discussion which should give you some clues as to the method for choosing the right answer:

When an employee has a complaint about his assignment, the action which will *best* help him overcome his difficulty is to
    A. discuss his difficulty with his coworkers
    B. take the problem to the head of the organization
    C. take the problem to the person who gave him the assignment
    D. say nothing to anyone about his complaint

In answering this question, you should study each of the choices to find which is best. Consider choice "A" – Certainly an employee may discuss his complaint with fellow employees, but no change or improvement can result, and the complaint remains unresolved. Choice "B" is a poor choice since the head of the organization probably does not know what assignment you have been given, and taking your problem to him is known as "going over the head" of the supervisor. The supervisor, or person who made the assignment, is the person who can clarify it or correct any injustice. Choice "C" is, therefore, correct. To say nothing, as in choice "D," is unwise. Supervisors have and interest in knowing the problems employees are facing, and the employee is seeking a solution to his problem.

2) True/False Questions

The "true/false" or "right/wrong" form of question is sometimes used. Here a complete statement is given. Your job is to decide whether the statement is right or wrong.

SAMPLE: A roaming cell-phone call to a nearby city costs less than a non-roaming call to a distant city.

This statement is wrong, or false, since roaming calls are more expensive.
This is not a complete list of all possible question forms, although most of the others are variations of these common types. You will always get complete directions for

answering questions. Be sure you understand *how* to mark your answers – ask questions until you do.

V. RECORDING YOUR ANSWERS

Computer terminals are used more and more today for many different kinds of exams.

For an examination with very few applicants, you may be told to record your answers in the test booklet itself. Separate answer sheets are much more common. If this separate answer sheet is to be scored by machine – and this is often the case – it is highly important that you mark your answers correctly in order to get credit.

An electronic scoring machine is often used in civil service offices because of the speed with which papers can be scored. Machine-scored answer sheets must be marked with a pencil, which will be given to you. This pencil has a high graphite content which responds to the electronic scoring machine. As a matter of fact, stray dots may register as answers, so do not let your pencil rest on the answer sheet while you are pondering the correct answer. Also, if your pencil lead breaks or is otherwise defective, ask for another.

Since the answer sheet will be dropped in a slot in the scoring machine, be careful not to bend the corners or get the paper crumpled.

The answer sheet normally has five vertical columns of numbers, with 30 numbers to a column. These numbers correspond to the question numbers in your test booklet. After each number, going across the page are four or five pairs of dotted lines. These short dotted lines have small letters or numbers above them. The first two pairs may also have a "T" or "F" above the letters. This indicates that the first two pairs only are to be used if the questions are of the true-false type. If the questions are multiple choice, disregard the "T" and "F" and pay attention only to the small letters or numbers.

Answer your questions in the manner of the sample that follows:

32. The largest city in the United States is
   A. Washington, D.C.
   B. New York City
   C. Chicago
   D. Detroit
   E. San Francisco

1) Choose the answer you think is best. (New York City is the largest, so "B" is correct.)
2) Find the row of dotted lines numbered the same as the question you are answering. (Find row number 32)
3) Find the pair of dotted lines corresponding to the answer. (Find the pair of lines under the mark "B.")
4) Make a solid black mark between the dotted lines.

VI. BEFORE THE TEST

Common sense will help you find procedures to follow to get ready for an examination. Too many of us, however, overlook these sensible measures. Indeed, nervousness and fatigue have been found to be the most serious reasons why applicants fail to do their best on civil service tests. Here is a list of reminders:

- Begin your preparation early – Don't wait until the last minute to go scurrying around for books and materials or to find out what the position is all about.
- Prepare continuously – An hour a night for a week is better than an all-night cram session. This has been definitely established. What is more, a night a week for a month will return better dividends than crowding your study into a shorter period of time.
- Locate the place of the exam – You have been sent a notice telling you when and where to report for the examination. If the location is in a different town or otherwise unfamiliar to you, it would be well to inquire the best route and learn something about the building.
- Relax the night before the test – Allow your mind to rest. Do not study at all that night. Plan some mild recreation or diversion; then go to bed early and get a good night's sleep.
- Get up early enough to make a leisurely trip to the place for the test – This way unforeseen events, traffic snarls, unfamiliar buildings, etc. will not upset you.
- Dress comfortably – A written test is not a fashion show. You will be known by number and not by name, so wear something comfortable.
- Leave excess paraphernalia at home – Shopping bags and odd bundles will get in your way. You need bring only the items mentioned in the official notice you received; usually everything you need is provided. Do not bring reference books to the exam. They will only confuse those last minutes and be taken away from you when in the test room.
- Arrive somewhat ahead of time – If because of transportation schedules you must get there very early, bring a newspaper or magazine to take your mind off yourself while waiting.
- Locate the examination room – When you have found the proper room, you will be directed to the seat or part of the room where you will sit. Sometimes you are given a sheet of instructions to read while you are waiting. Do not fill out any forms until you are told to do so; just read them and be prepared.
- Relax and prepare to listen to the instructions
- If you have any physical problem that may keep you from doing your best, be sure to tell the test administrator. If you are sick or in poor health, you really cannot do your best on the exam. You can come back and take the test some other time.

VII. AT THE TEST

The day of the test is here and you have the test booklet in your hand. The temptation to get going is very strong. Caution! There is more to success than knowing the right answers. You must know how to identify your papers and understand variations in the type of short-answer question used in this particular examination. Follow these suggestions for maximum results from your efforts:

1) Cooperate with the monitor

The test administrator has a duty to create a situation in which you can be as much at ease as possible. He will give instructions, tell you when to begin, check to see that you are marking your answer sheet correctly, and so on. He is not there to guard you, although he will see that your competitors do not take unfair advantage. He wants to help you do your best.

2) Listen to all instructions

Don't jump the gun! Wait until you understand all directions. In most civil service tests you get more time than you need to answer the questions. So don't be in a hurry. Read each word of instructions until you clearly understand the meaning. Study the examples, listen to all announcements and follow directions. Ask questions if you do not understand what to do.

3) Identify your papers

Civil service exams are usually identified by number only. You will be assigned a number; you must not put your name on your test papers. Be sure to copy your number correctly. Since more than one exam may be given, copy your exact examination title.

4) Plan your time

Unless you are told that a test is a "speed" or "rate of work" test, speed itself is usually not important. Time enough to answer all the questions will be provided, but this does not mean that you have all day. An overall time limit has been set. Divide the total time (in minutes) by the number of questions to determine the approximate time you have for each question.

5) Do not linger over difficult questions

If you come across a difficult question, mark it with a paper clip (useful to have along) and come back to it when you have been through the booklet. One caution if you do this – be sure to skip a number on your answer sheet as well. Check often to be sure that you have not lost your place and that you are marking in the row numbered the same as the question you are answering.

6) Read the questions

Be sure you know what the question asks! Many capable people are unsuccessful because they failed to *read* the questions correctly.

7) Answer all questions

Unless you have been instructed that a penalty will be deducted for incorrect answers, it is better to guess than to omit a question.

8) Speed tests

It is often better NOT to guess on speed tests. It has been found that on timed tests people are tempted to spend the last few seconds before time is called in marking answers at random – without even reading them – in the hope of picking up a few extra points. To discourage this practice, the instructions may warn you that your score will be "corrected" for guessing. That is, a penalty will be applied. The incorrect answers will be deducted from the correct ones, or some other penalty formula will be used.

9) Review your answers

If you finish before time is called, go back to the questions you guessed or omitted to give them further thought. Review other answers if you have time.

10) Return your test materials

If you are ready to leave before others have finished or time is called, take ALL your materials to the monitor and leave quietly. Never take any test material with you. The monitor can discover whose papers are not complete, and taking a test booklet may be grounds for disqualification.

VIII. EXAMINATION TECHNIQUES

1) Read the general instructions carefully. These are usually printed on the first page of the exam booklet. As a rule, these instructions refer to the timing of the examination; the fact that you should not start work until the signal and must stop work at a signal, etc. If there are any *special* instructions, such as a choice of questions to be answered, make sure that you note this instruction carefully.

2) When you are ready to start work on the examination, that is as soon as the signal has been given, read the instructions to each question booklet, underline any key words or phrases, such as *least, best, outline, describe* and the like. In this way you will tend to answer as requested rather than discover on reviewing your paper that you *listed without describing*, that you selected the *worst* choice rather than the *best* choice, etc.

3) If the examination is of the objective or multiple-choice type – that is, each question will also give a series of possible answers: A, B, C or D, and you are called upon to select the best answer and write the letter next to that answer on your answer paper – it is advisable to start answering each question in turn. There may be anywhere from 50 to 100 such questions in the three or four hours allotted and you can see how much time would be taken if you read through all the questions before beginning to answer any. Furthermore, if you come across a question or group of questions which you know would be difficult to answer, it would undoubtedly affect your handling of all the other questions.

4) If the examination is of the essay type and contains but a few questions, it is a moot point as to whether you should read all the questions before starting to answer any one. Of course, if you are given a choice – say five out of seven and the like – then it is essential to read all the questions so you can eliminate the two that are most difficult. If, however, you are asked to answer all the questions, there may be danger in trying to answer the easiest one first because you may find that you will spend too much time on it. The best technique is to answer the first question, then proceed to the second, etc.

5) Time your answers. Before the exam begins, write down the time it started, then add the time allowed for the examination and write down the time it must be completed, then divide the time available somewhat as follows:

- If 3-1/2 hours are allowed, that would be 210 minutes. If you have 80 objective-type questions, that would be an average of 2-1/2 minutes per question. Allow yourself no more than 2 minutes per question, or a total of 160 minutes, which will permit about 50 minutes to review.
- If for the time allotment of 210 minutes there are 7 essay questions to answer, that would average about 30 minutes a question. Give yourself only 25 minutes per question so that you have about 35 minutes to review.

6) The most important instruction is to *read each question* and make sure you know what is wanted. The second most important instruction is to *time yourself properly* so that you answer every question. The third most important instruction is to *answer every question*. Guess if you have to but include something for each question. Remember that you will receive no credit for a blank and will probably receive some credit if you write something in answer to an essay question. If you guess a letter – say "B" for a multiple-choice question – you may have guessed right. If you leave a blank as an answer to a multiple-choice question, the examiners may respect your feelings but it will not add a point to your score. Some exams may penalize you for wrong answers, so in such cases *only*, you may not want to guess unless you have some basis for your answer.

7) Suggestions
   a. Objective-type questions
      1. Examine the question booklet for proper sequence of pages and questions
      2. Read all instructions carefully
      3. Skip any question which seems too difficult; return to it after all other questions have been answered
      4. Apportion your time properly; do not spend too much time on any single question or group of questions
      5. Note and underline key words – *all, most, fewest, least, best, worst, same, opposite,* etc.
      6. Pay particular attention to negatives
      7. Note unusual option, e.g., unduly long, short, complex, different or similar in content to the body of the question
      8. Observe the use of "hedging" words – *probably, may, most likely*, etc.
      9. Make sure that your answer is put next to the same number as the question
      10. Do not second-guess unless you have good reason to believe the second answer is definitely more correct
      11. Cross out original answer if you decide another answer is more accurate; do not erase until you are ready to hand your paper in
      12. Answer all questions; guess unless instructed otherwise
      13. Leave time for review

   b. Essay questions
      1. Read each question carefully
      2. Determine exactly what is wanted. Underline key words or phrases.
      3. Decide on outline or paragraph answer

4. Include many different points and elements unless asked to develop any one or two points or elements
5. Show impartiality by giving pros and cons unless directed to select one side only
6. Make and write down any assumptions you find necessary to answer the questions
7. Watch your English, grammar, punctuation and choice of words
8. Time your answers; don't crowd material

8) Answering the essay question

Most essay questions can be answered by framing the specific response around several key words or ideas. Here are a few such key words or ideas:

M's: manpower, materials, methods, money, management
P's: purpose, program, policy, plan, procedure, practice, problems, pitfalls, personnel, public relations
   a. Six basic steps in handling problems:
      1. Preliminary plan and background development
      2. Collect information, data and facts
      3. Analyze and interpret information, data and facts
      4. Analyze and develop solutions as well as make recommendations
      5. Prepare report and sell recommendations
      6. Install recommendations and follow up effectiveness

   b. Pitfalls to avoid
      1. *Taking things for granted* – A statement of the situation does not necessarily imply that each of the elements is necessarily true; for example, a complaint may be invalid and biased so that all that can be taken for granted is that a complaint has been registered
      2. *Considering only one side of a situation* – Wherever possible, indicate several alternatives and then point out the reasons you selected the best one
      3. *Failing to indicate follow up* – Whenever your answer indicates action on your part, make certain that you will take proper follow-up action to see how successful your recommendations, procedures or actions turn out to be
      4. *Taking too long in answering any single question* – Remember to time your answers properly

IX. AFTER THE TEST

Scoring procedures differ in detail among civil service jurisdictions although the general principles are the same. Whether the papers are hand-scored or graded by machine we have described, they are nearly always graded by number. That is, the person who marks the paper knows only the number – never the name – of the applicant. Not until all the papers have been graded will they be matched with names. If other tests, such as training and experience or oral interview ratings have been given, scores will be combined. Different parts of the examination usually have different weights. For example, the written test might count 60 percent of the final grade, and a rating of training and experience 40 percent. In many jurisdictions, veterans will have a certain number of points added to their grades.

After the final grade has been determined, the names are placed in grade order and an eligible list is established. There are various methods for resolving ties between those who get the same final grade – probably the most common is to place first the name of the person whose application was received first. Job offers are made from the eligible list in the order the names appear on it. You will be notified of your grade and your rank as soon as all these computations have been made. This will be done as rapidly as possible.

People who are found to meet the requirements in the announcement are called "eligibles." Their names are put on a list of eligible candidates. An eligible's chances of getting a job depend on how high he stands on this list and how fast agencies are filling jobs from the list.

When a job is to be filled from a list of eligibles, the agency asks for the names of people on the list of eligibles for that job. When the civil service commission receives this request, it sends to the agency the names of the three people highest on this list. Or, if the job to be filled has specialized requirements, the office sends the agency the names of the top three persons who meet these requirements from the general list.

The appointing officer makes a choice from among the three people whose names were sent to him. If the selected person accepts the appointment, the names of the others are put back on the list to be considered for future openings.

That is the rule in hiring from all kinds of eligible lists, whether they are for typist, carpenter, chemist, or something else. For every vacancy, the appointing officer has his choice of any one of the top three eligibles on the list. This explains why the person whose name is on top of the list sometimes does not get an appointment when some of the persons lower on the list do. If the appointing officer chooses the second or third eligible, the No. 1 eligible does not get a job at once, but stays on the list until he is appointed or the list is terminated.

X. HOW TO PASS THE INTERVIEW TEST

The examination for which you applied requires an oral interview test. You have already taken the written test and you are now being called for the interview test – the final part of the formal examination.

You may think that it is not possible to prepare for an interview test and that there are no procedures to follow during an interview. Our purpose is to point out some things you can do in advance that will help you and some good rules to follow and pitfalls to avoid while you are being interviewed.

What is an interview supposed to test?

The written examination is designed to test the technical knowledge and competence of the candidate; the oral is designed to evaluate intangible qualities, not readily measured otherwise, and to establish a list showing the relative fitness of each candidate – as measured against his competitors – for the position sought. Scoring is not on the basis of "right" and "wrong," but on a sliding scale of values ranging from "not passable" to "outstanding." As a matter of fact, it is possible to achieve a relatively low score without a single "incorrect" answer because of evident weakness in the qualities being measured.

Occasionally, an examination may consist entirely of an oral test – either an individual or a group oral. In such cases, information is sought concerning the technical knowledges and abilities of the candidate, since there has been no written examination for this purpose. More commonly, however, an oral test is used to supplement a written examination.

Who conducts interviews?

The composition of oral boards varies among different jurisdictions. In nearly all, a representative of the personnel department serves as chairman. One of the members of the board may be a representative of the department in which the candidate would work. In some cases, "outside experts" are used, and, frequently, a businessman or some other representative of the general public is asked to serve. Labor and management or other special groups may be represented. The aim is to secure the services of experts in the appropriate field.

However the board is composed, it is a good idea (and not at all improper or unethical) to ascertain in advance of the interview who the members are and what groups they represent. When you are introduced to them, you will have some idea of their backgrounds and interests, and at least you will not stutter and stammer over their names.

What should be done before the interview?

While knowledge about the board members is useful and takes some of the surprise element out of the interview, there is other preparation which is more substantive. It *is* possible to prepare for an oral interview – in several ways:

1) Keep a copy of your application and review it carefully before the interview

This may be the only document before the oral board, and the starting point of the interview. Know what education and experience you have listed there, and the sequence and dates of all of it. Sometimes the board will ask you to review the highlights of your experience for them; you should not have to hem and haw doing it.

2) Study the class specification and the examination announcement

Usually, the oral board has one or both of these to guide them. The qualities, characteristics or knowledges required by the position sought are stated in these documents. They offer valuable clues as to the nature of the oral interview. For example, if the job involves supervisory responsibilities, the announcement will usually indicate that knowledge of modern supervisory methods and the qualifications of the candidate as a supervisor will be tested. If so, you can expect such questions, frequently in the form of a hypothetical situation which you are expected to solve. NEVER go into an oral without knowledge of the duties and responsibilities of the job you seek.

3) Think through each qualification required

Try to visualize the kind of questions you would ask if you were a board member. How well could you answer them? Try especially to appraise your own knowledge and background in each area, *measured against the job sought*, and identify any areas in which you are weak. Be critical and realistic – do not flatter yourself.

4) Do some general reading in areas in which you feel you may be weak

For example, if the job involves supervision and your past experience has NOT, some general reading in supervisory methods and practices, particularly in the field of human relations, might be useful. Do NOT study agency procedures or detailed manuals. The oral board will be testing your understanding and capacity, not your memory.

5) Get a good night's sleep and watch your general health and mental attitude

You will want a clear head at the interview. Take care of a cold or any other minor ailment, and of course, no hangovers.

What should be done on the day of the interview?

Now comes the day of the interview itself. Give yourself plenty of time to get there. Plan to arrive somewhat ahead of the scheduled time, particularly if your appointment is in the fore part of the day. If a previous candidate fails to appear, the board might be ready for you a bit early. By early afternoon an oral board is almost invariably behind schedule if there are many candidates, and you may have to wait. Take along a book or magazine to read, or your application to review, but leave any extraneous material in the waiting room when you go in for your interview. In any event, relax and compose yourself.

The matter of dress is important. The board is forming impressions about you – from your experience, your manners, your attitude, and your appearance. Give your personal appearance careful attention. Dress your best, but not your flashiest. Choose conservative, appropriate clothing, and be sure it is immaculate. This is a business interview, and your appearance should indicate that you regard it as such. Besides, being well groomed and properly dressed will help boost your confidence.

Sooner or later, someone will call your name and escort you into the interview room. *This is it.* From here on you are on your own. It is too late for any more preparation. But remember, you asked for this opportunity to prove your fitness, and you are here because your request was granted.

What happens when you go in?

The usual sequence of events will be as follows: The clerk (who is often the board stenographer) will introduce you to the chairman of the oral board, who will introduce you to the other members of the board. Acknowledge the introductions before you sit down. Do not be surprised if you find a microphone facing you or a stenotypist sitting by. Oral interviews are usually recorded in the event of an appeal or other review.

Usually the chairman of the board will open the interview by reviewing the highlights of your education and work experience from your application – primarily for the benefit of the other members of the board, as well as to get the material into the record. Do not interrupt or comment unless there is an error or significant misinterpretation; if that is the case, do not hesitate. But do not quibble about insignificant matters. Also, he will usually ask you some question about your education, experience or your present job – partly to get you to start talking and to establish the interviewing "rapport." He may start the actual questioning, or turn it over to one of the other members. Frequently, each member undertakes the questioning on a particular area, one in which he is perhaps most competent, so you can expect each member to participate in the examination. Because time is limited, you may also expect some rather abrupt switches in the direction the questioning takes, so do not be upset by it. Normally, a board member will not pursue a single line of questioning unless he discovers a particular strength or weakness.

After each member has participated, the chairman will usually ask whether any member has any further questions, then will ask you if you have anything you wish to add. Unless you are expecting this question, it may floor you. Worse, it may start you off on an extended, extemporaneous speech. The board is not usually seeking more information. The question is principally to offer you a last opportunity to present further qualifications or to indicate that you have nothing to add. So, if you feel that a significant qualification or characteristic has been overlooked, it is proper to point it out in a sentence or so. Do not compliment the board on the thoroughness of their examination – they have been sketchy, and you know it. If you wish, merely say, "No thank you, I have nothing further to add." This is a point where you can "talk yourself out" of a good impression or fail to present an important bit of information. Remember, *you close the interview yourself.*

The chairman will then say, "That is all, Mr. _____, thank you." Do not be startled; the interview is over, and quicker than you think. Thank him, gather your belongings and take your leave. Save your sigh of relief for the other side of the door.

How to put your best foot forward

Throughout this entire process, you may feel that the board individually and collectively is trying to pierce your defenses, seek out your hidden weaknesses and embarrass and confuse you. Actually, this is not true. They are obliged to make an appraisal of your qualifications for the job you are seeking, and they want to see you in your best light. Remember, they must interview all candidates and a non-cooperative candidate may become a failure in spite of their best efforts to bring out his qualifications. Here are 15 suggestions that will help you:

1) Be natural – Keep your attitude confident, not cocky

If you are not confident that you can do the job, do not expect the board to be. Do not apologize for your weaknesses, try to bring out your strong points. The board is interested in a positive, not negative, presentation. Cockiness will antagonize any board member and make him wonder if you are covering up a weakness by a false show of strength.

2) Get comfortable, but don't lounge or sprawl

Sit erectly but not stiffly. A careless posture may lead the board to conclude that you are careless in other things, or at least that you are not impressed by the importance of the occasion. Either conclusion is natural, even if incorrect. Do not fuss with your clothing, a pencil or an ashtray. Your hands may occasionally be useful to emphasize a point; do not let them become a point of distraction.

3) Do not wisecrack or make small talk

This is a serious situation, and your attitude should show that you consider it as such. Further, the time of the board is limited – they do not want to waste it, and neither should you.

4) Do not exaggerate your experience or abilities

In the first place, from information in the application or other interviews and sources, the board may know more about you than you think. Secondly, you probably will not get away with it. An experienced board is rather adept at spotting such a situation, so do not take the chance.

5) If you know a board member, do not make a point of it, yet do not hide it

Certainly you are not fooling him, and probably not the other members of the board. Do not try to take advantage of your acquaintanceship – it will probably do you little good.

6) Do not dominate the interview

Let the board do that. They will give you the clues – do not assume that you have to do all the talking. Realize that the board has a number of questions to ask you, and do not try to take up all the interview time by showing off your extensive knowledge of the answer to the first one.

7) Be attentive

You only have 20 minutes or so, and you should keep your attention at its sharpest throughout. When a member is addressing a problem or question to you, give him your undivided attention. Address your reply principally to him, but do not exclude the other board members.

8) Do not interrupt

A board member may be stating a problem for you to analyze. He will ask you a question when the time comes. Let him state the problem, and wait for the question.

9) Make sure you understand the question

Do not try to answer until you are sure what the question is. If it is not clear, restate it in your own words or ask the board member to clarify it for you. However, do not haggle about minor elements.

10) Reply promptly but not hastily

A common entry on oral board rating sheets is "candidate responded readily," or "candidate hesitated in replies." Respond as promptly and quickly as you can, but do not jump to a hasty, ill-considered answer.

11) Do not be peremptory in your answers

A brief answer is proper – but do not fire your answer back. That is a losing game from your point of view. The board member can probably ask questions much faster than you can answer them.

12) Do not try to create the answer you think the board member wants

He is interested in what kind of mind you have and how it works – not in playing games. Furthermore, he can usually spot this practice and will actually grade you down on it.

13) Do not switch sides in your reply merely to agree with a board member

Frequently, a member will take a contrary position merely to draw you out and to see if you are willing and able to defend your point of view. Do not start a debate, yet do not surrender a good position. If a position is worth taking, it is worth defending.

14) Do not be afraid to admit an error in judgment if you are shown to be wrong
   The board knows that you are forced to reply without any opportunity for careful consideration. Your answer may be demonstrably wrong. If so, admit it and get on with the interview.

15) Do not dwell at length on your present job
   The opening question may relate to your present assignment. Answer the question but do not go into an extended discussion. You are being examined for a *new* job, not your present one. As a matter of fact, try to phrase ALL your answers in terms of the job for which you are being examined.

Basis of Rating
   Probably you will forget most of these "do's" and "don'ts" when you walk into the oral interview room. Even remembering them all will not ensure you a passing grade. Perhaps you did not have the qualifications in the first place. But remembering them will help you to put your best foot forward, without treading on the toes of the board members.
   Rumor and popular opinion to the contrary notwithstanding, an oral board wants you to make the best appearance possible. They know you are under pressure – but they also want to see how you respond to it as a guide to what your reaction would be under the pressures of the job you seek. They will be influenced by the degree of poise you display, the personal traits you show and the manner in which you respond.

ABOUT THIS BOOK

   This book contains tests divided into Examination Sections. Go through each test, answering every question in the margin. At the end of each test look at the answer key and check your answers. On the ones you got wrong, look at the right answer choice and learn. Do not fill in the answers first. Do not memorize the questions and answers, but understand the answer and principles involved. On your test, the questions will likely be different from the samples. Questions are changed and new ones added. If you understand these past questions you should have success with any changes that arise. Tests may consist of several types of questions. We have additional books on each subject should more study be advisable or necessary for you. Finally, the more you study, the better prepared you will be. This book is intended to be the last thing you study before you walk into the examination room. Prior study of relevant texts is also recommended. NLC publishes some of these in our Fundamental Series. Knowledge and good sense are important factors in passing your exam. Good luck also helps. So now study this Passbook, absorb the material contained within and take that knowledge into the examination. Then do your best to pass that exam.

EXAMINATION SECTION

EXAMINATION SECTION
TEST 1

DIRECTIONS: Each question or incomplete statement is followed by several suggested answers or completions. Select the one that BEST answers the question or completes the statement. *PRINT THE LETTER OF THE CORRECT ANSWER IN THE SPACE AT THE RIGHT.*

1. During the course of our examination of the financial statements of The Angel Co., a new client, for the year ended December 31, 2015, you discover the following:
   - Inventory at January 1, 2015 had been overstated by $3,000.
   - Inventory at December 31, 2015 was understated by $5,000.
   - An insurance policy covering three years had been purchased on January 2, 2014 for $1,500. The entire amount was charged as an expense in 2014.
   - During 2015, the company received a $1,000 cash advance from a customer for merchandise to be manufactured and shipped during 2016. The $1,000 had been credited to sales revenue. The company's gross profit on sales is 50%.
   - Net income reported on the 2015 income statement (before reflecting any adjustments for the above items) is $20,000.

   The proper net income for 2015 is
   A. $26,500   B. $23,500   C. $16,500   D. $20,500

   1.____

2. Guille, Inc. received a $600, 90-day, 5% note from a customer in payment for the purchase of merchandise. Guille, Inc. immediately discounted the note at a bank at a 6% discount rate. The proceeds received by Guille, Inc. on discounting the note amounted to
   A. $607.50   B. $590.89   C. $58.39   D. $616.61

   2.____

3. A company's profit-sharing plan provides that the company will contribute to a fund an amount equal to one-third of its net income after taxes each year. Income before taxes and before deducting the profit-sharing contribution for 2015 is $600,000. The applicable income tax rate is 40%. The amount to be contributed to the profit-sharing fund for 2015 is
   A. $200,000   B. $120,000   C. $100,000   D. $133,333

   3.____

4. The Harsch Company provides an incentive compensation plan under which its president is to receive a bonus equal to 10% of the company's income in excess of $100,000 before deducting income tax but after deducting the bonus. If income before income tax and bonus is $320,000 and the effective tax rate is 40%, the amount of the bonus should be
   A. $20,000   B. $22,000   C. $32,000   D. $44,000

   4.____

Questions 5-6.

DIRECTIONS: Questions 5 and 6 are to be answered on the basis of the following information.

The following balance sheet is for the partnership of A, B, and C, which shares profits and losses in the ration of 4:4:2, respectively.

Assets

Cash	$20,000
Other assets	180,000
	$200,000

Liabilities and Capital

Liabilities	$50,000
A, Capital	37,000
B, Capital	65,000
C, Capital	$200,000

5. The original partnership was dissolved when its assets, liabilities, and capital were as shown on the above balance sheet and liquidated by selling assets in installments. The first sale of non-cash assets having a book value of $90,000 realized $50,000, and all cash available after settlement with creditors was distributed. How much cash should the respective partners receive (to the nearest dollar)?
A _____ ; B _____ ; C _____.
  A. $8,000; $8,000; $4,000
  B. $6,667; $6,667; $6,666
  C. $0; $13,333; $6,667
  D. $0; $3,000; $17,000

5.____

6. Independent of Question 5 above, assume that the assets and liabilities are fairly valued on the above balance sheet. The partnership wishes to admit Knight as a partner with a one-sixth interest without recording goodwill or bonus. What amount of cash or other assets should Knight contribute?
  A. $30,000   B. $33,333   C. $36,000   D. $40,000

6.____

Questions 7-11.

DIRECTIONS: Questions 7 through 11 are to be answered on the basis of the following information.

The following data relate to a year's budgeting activity for Hardrock Corporation, a single-product company.

	Units
Beginning inventory	30,000
Production	120,000
Available	150,000
Sales	110,000
Ending inventory	40,000

	Per Unit
Selling price	$5.00
Variable manufacturing costs	1.00
Variable selling costs	2.00
Fixed manufacturing costs (based on 100,000 units)	.25
Fixed selling costs (based on 100,000 units)	.65

The total fixed costs remain unchanged within the relevant range of 25,000 units to total capacity of 160,000 units.

7. The projected annual break-even sales in units for Hardrock Corporation is
   A. 30,000   B. 37,143   C. 45,000   D. 50,000

8. The projected net income for Hardrock Corporation for the year under direct (variable) costing is
   A. $110,000   B. $127,500   C. $130,000   D. $150,000

9. If all the variances are charged to cost of goods sold, the projected net income for Hardrock Corporation for the year under absorption costing is
   A. $122,500   B. $127,500   C. $130,000   D. $132,500

10. A special order is received to purchase 10,000 units to be used in an unrelated market. Given the original data, what price per unit should be charged on this order to INCREASE Hardrock Corporation's net income by $5,000?
    A. $3.50   B. $4.40   C. $5.00   D. $6.50

11. Concerning the data for Hardrock Corporation, assume selling price increases by 20%; variable manufacturing costs increase by 10%; variable selling costs remain the same; and total fixed costs increase to $104,400. How many units must now be sold to generate a profit equal to 10% of the contribution margin?
    A. 36,000   B. 40,000   C. 43,320   D. 45,390

12. The term *relevant range*, as used in cost accounting, means the range
    A. over which costs may fluctuate
    B. over which cost relationships are valid
    C. of probable production
    D. over which relevant costs are incurred

4 (#1)

13. The method of accounting for joint-product costs that will produce the same gross-profit rate for all products is the _____ method.
    A. relative sales-value
    B. physical-measure
    C. actual-costing
    D. services-received

13._____

14. The concept of *management by exception* refers to management's
    A. consideration of only those items which vary materially from plans
    B. consideration of only rare events
    C. consideration of items selected at random
    D. lack of a pre-determined plan

14._____

15. Under a job-order system of cost accounting, the dollar amount of the entry involved in the transfer of inventory from work-in-process to finished goods is the sum of the costs charged to all jobs _____ during the period.
    A. started in process
    B. in process
    C. completed and sold
    D. completed

15._____

16. If over- or under-applied overhead is interpreted as an error in allocating actual costs against the production of the year, this suggests that the over- or under-applied overhead of this year should be
    A. carried forward in the overhead control account from year to year
    B. eliminated by changing the predetermined overhead rate in subsequent years
    C. apportioned among the work-in-process inventory, the finished goods inventory, and the cost of goods sold
    D. treated as a special gain or loss occurring during this year

16._____

17. The budget variance for fixed factory overhead for the normal-volume, practical-capacity, and expected-activity levels would be the same
    A. except for normal volume
    B. except for practical capacity
    C. except for expected activity
    D. for all three activity levels

17._____

Questions 18-20.

DIRECTIONS: Questions 18 through 20 are to be answered on the basis of the following information.

Marlborough Retail seeks your assistance to develop cash and other budget information for May, June, and July 2015. At April 30, 2015, the company had cash of $5,500, accounts receivable of $437,000, inventories of $309,400, and accounts payable of $133,055.

The budget is to be based on the following assumptions:

5 (#1)

I. Sales
   a. Each month's sales are billed on the last day of the month.
   b. Customers are allowed a 3% discount if payment is made within ten days after the billing date. Receivable are booked gross.
   c. Sixty percent of the bills are collected within the discount period, 25% are collected by the end of the month, 9% are collected by the end of the second month, and 6% prove uncollectible.

II. Purchases
   a. Fifty-four percent of all purchases of material and selling, general, and administrative expenses are paid in the month purchased and the remainder in the following month.
   b. Each month's units of ending inventory is equal to 130% of the next month's units of sales.
   c. The cost of each unit of inventory is $20.
   d. Selling, general, and administrative expenses. of which $2,000 is depreciation, are equal to 15% of the current month's sales.

Actual and projected sales are as follows:

2015	Dollars	Units
March	$354,000	11,800
April	363,000	12,100
May	357,000	11,900
June	342,000	11,400
July	360,000	12,000
August	366,000	12,200

18. Budgeting cash disbursements during the month of June 2015 are
    A. $292,900   B. $287,370   C. $294,900   D. $285,379

19. Budgeted cash collections during the month of May 2015 are
    A. $333,876   B. $355,116   C. 340,410   D. $355,656

20. The budgeting number of units of inventory to be purchased during July 2015 is
    A. 15,860   B. 12,260   C. 12,000   D. 15,600

KEY (CORRECT ANSWERS)

1.	A	11.	B
2.	C	12.	B
3.	C	13.	A
4.	A	14.	A
5.	D	15.	D
6.	A	16.	C
7.	C	17.	D
8.	C	18.	D
9.	D	19.	A
10.	A	20.	B

TEST 2

DIRECTIONS: Each question or incomplete statement is followed by several suggested answers or completions. Select the one that BEST answers the question or completes the statement. *PRINT THE LETTER OF THE CORRECT ANSWER IN THE SPACE AT THE RIGHT.*

Questions 1-4.

DIRECTIONS: Questions 1 through 4 are to be answered on the basis of the following information.

The Yanqui Manufacturing Company has two production departments (fabrication and assembly) and three service departments (general factory administration, factory maintenance, and factory cafeteria). A summary of costs and other data for each department prior to allocation of service-department costs for the year ended June 30, 2015 appears below.

The costs of the general factory administration department, factory maintenance department, and factory cafeteria are allocated on the basis of direct-labor hours, square-footage occupied, and number of employees, respectively. There are no manufacturing-overhead variances. Round all final calculations to the nearest dollar.

	Fabrication	Assembly	General Factory Administration	Factory Maintenance	Factory Cafeteria
Direct-labor costs	$1,950,000	$2,050,000	$90,000	$82,100	$87,000
Direct-material costs	$3,130,000	$950,000	-	$65,000	$91,000
Manufacturing-overhead costs	$1,650,000	$1,850,000	$70,000	$56,100	$62,000
Direct-labor hours	562,500	437,500	31,000	27,000	42,000
Number of employees	280	200	12	8	20
Square-footage occupied	88,000	72,000	1,750	2,000	4,800

1. Assuming that Yanqui elects to distribute service-department costs directly to production departments without inter-service department cost allocation, the amount of factory-maintenance department costs which would be allocated to the fabrication department would be
 A. $0 B. $111,760 C. $106,091 D. $91,440

 1.____

2. Assuming the same method of allocation as in Question 1 above, the amount of general factory administration department costs which would be allocated to the assembly department would be
 A. $0 B. $63,636 C. $70,000 D. $90,000

 2.____

3. Assuming that Yanqui elects to distribute service-department costs to other service departments (starting with the service department with the greatest total costs), as well as the production departments, the amount of factory cafeteria department costs which would be allocated to the factory maintenance department would be (Note: Once a service department's costs have been reallocated, no subsequent service-department costs are recirculated back to it.)
   A. $0 B. $96,000 C. $3,840 D. $6,124

4. Assuming the same method of allocation as in Question 3 above, the amount of factory maintenance department costs which would be allocated to the factory cafeteria would be
   A. $0 B. $5,787 C. $5,856 D. $148,910

5. Total production costs for Slow, Inc. are budgeted at $230,000 for 50,000 units of budgeted output and at $280,000 for 60,000 units of budgeted output. Because of the need for additional facilities, budgeted fixed costs for 60,000 units are 25% more than budgeted fixed costs for 50,000 units. How much is Slow's budgeted variable cost per unit of output?
   A. $1.60 B. $1.67 C. $3.00 D. $5.00

6. Which one of the following notations represents the first half-year's depreciation on a new asset using the sum-of-the-years'-digits depreciation method, a fifty-year life, and a cost (net of salvage) of $40,000?

   A. $\$40{,}000 \times (25 \div \sum_{Y=1}^{25} Y)$

   B. $\$40{,}000 \times (25 \div \sum_{Y=1}^{50} Y)$

   C. $\$40{,}000 \times (50 \div \sum_{Y=1}^{25} Y)$

   D. $\$40{,}000 \times (50 \div \sum_{Y=1}^{50} Y)$

7. Your client, a charity, is planning a carnival to raise money. The charity has permission from the local authorities to have games of chance. For one of these games, the player draws one card from a standard deck of 52 cards. If the player draws a jack of hearts, jack of diamonds, or jack of spades, he is paid $6.50. If he draws any card of clubs, he is paid $2.50. Assume X equals the price your client should charge per draw so that the long-run expected value of this game is zero. Which one of the following equations should be used to determine that price?
   A. 3/52(6.50-X) + 13/52(.50-X) = X
   B. 3/32(6.50-X) + 13/52(2.50-X) = 36/52X
   C. 3/52(6.50) + 13/52(2.50) = 36/52X
   D. 6.50 – 2.50 = 36/52X

Questions 8-9.

DIRECTIONS: Questions 8 and 9 are to be answered on the basis of the following information.

The Silver Lamb Manufacturing Company wants to maximize the profits in products A, B, and C. The contribution margin for each product follows:

Product	Contribution Margin
A	$2
B	$5
C	$4

The production requirements and departmental capacities, by departments, are as follows:

Department	Production Requirements By Product (Hours)		
	A	B	C
Assembling	2	3	2
Painting	1	2	2
Finishing	2	3	1

Department	Departmental Capacity (Total Hours)
Assembling	30,000
Painting	38,000
Finishing	28,000

8. What is the profit-maximization formula for the Silver Lamb Company?
    A. $2A + $5B + $4C = X (where X = profit)
    B. 5A + 8B + 5C ≤ 96,000
    C. $2A + $5B + $4C ≤ X (where X = profit)
    D. $2A + $5B + $4C = 96,000

9. What is the constraint for the Painting Department of the Silver Lamb Company?
    A. 1A + 2B + 2C ≥ 38,000
    B. $2A + $5B + $4C ≥ 38,000
    C. 1A + 2B + 2C ≤ 38,000
    D. 2A + 3B + 2C ≤ 38,000

10. A company employing very tight (high) standards in a standard-cost system should expect that
    A. no incentive bonus will be paid
    B. most variances will be unfavorable
    C. employees will be strongly motivated to attain the standards
    D. costs will be controlled better than if lower standards were used

11. Standard costing will produce the same financial statement results as actual or conventional costing when standard-cost variances are distributed to
    A. cost of goods sold
    B. an income or expense account
    C. cost of goods sold and inventory
    D. a balance sheet account

12. A spending variance for variable overhead based on direct labor hours is the difference between actual variable overhead cost and variable overhead cost that should have been incurred for the actual hours worked, and results from
    A. price and quantity differences for overhead costs
    B. price differences for overhead costs
    C. quantity differences for overhead costs
    D. differences caused by variations in production volume

13. The cost-volume-profit analysis underlying the conventional break-even chart does NOT assume that
    A. prices will remain fixed
    B. production will equal sales
    C. some costs vary inversely with volume
    D. costs are linear and continuous over the relevant range

14. The PRIMARY difference between a fixed budget and a variable (flexible) budget is that a fixed budget _____, while a variable budget _____.
    A. includes only fixed costs; includes only variable costs
    B. is concerned only with future acquisitions of fixed assets; is concerned with expenses which vary with sales
    C. cannot be changed after the period begins; can be changed after the period begins
    D. is a plan for a single level of sales (or other measure of activity); consists of several plans, one for each of several levels (or other measure of activity)

15. Sapp Co. provides an allowance for its doubtful accounts receivable. At December 31, 2014, the allowance account had a credit balance of $2,000. Each month, Sapp Co. accrues bad-debt expense in an amount equal to 1% of sales on account. Total sales on account during 2015 amounted to $500,000. During 2015, accounts receivable totaling $8,000 were written off as worthless. An aging of accounts receivable at December 31, 2015 indicates tha an allowance of $10,000 should be provided for doubtful accounts as of that date. Accordingly, bad-debt expense previously accrued during 2015 should be increased by
    A. $10,000   B. $11,000   C. $1,000   D. $13,000

16. Crary Co. prepares monthly income statements. A physical inventory is taken only at year-end, hence month-end inventories must be estimated. All sales are made on account. The rate of mark-up on cost is 50%. The following information relates to the month of June 2015:

Accounts receivable, June 1, 2015	$10,000
Accounts receivable, June 30, 2015	15,000
Collection of accounts receivable during June 2015	25,000
Inventory, June 1, 2015	18,000
Purchases of inventory during June 2015	16,000

    The estimated cost of the June 30, 2015 inventory would be
    A. $12,000   B. $14,000   C. $19,000   D. $22,000

5 (#2)

17. The receipts from a special tax levy to retire and pay interest on general obligation bonds issued to finance the construction of a new city hall should be recorded in a _____ fund.   17.____
    A. debt service
    B. capital projects
    C. revolving interest
    D. special revenue
    E. none of the above

18. The operations of a municipal swimming pool receiving the majority of its support from charges to users should be accounted for in _____ fund.   18.____
    A. a special revenue
    B. the general
    C. an intragovernmental service
    D. an enterprise
    E. none of the above

19. The fixed assets of a central purchasing and stores department organized to serve all municipal departments should be recorded in   19.____
    A. an enterprise fund and the general fixed assets group
    B. an enterprise fund
    C. the general fixed assets group
    D. the general fund
    E. none of the above

20. The monthly remittance to an insurance company of the lump sum of hospital-surgical insurance premiums collected as payroll deductions from employees should be recorded in _____ fund.   20.____
    A. the general
    B. an agency
    C. a special revenue
    D. an intragovernmental service
    E. none of the above

KEY (CORRECT ANSWERS)

1.	B	11.	C
2.	C	12.	B
3.	C	13.	C
4.	A	14.	D
5.	C	15.	B
6.	B	16.	B
7.	B	17.	A
8.	A	18.	D
9.	C	19.	E
10.	B	20.	B

EXAMINATION SECTION
TEST 3

DIRECTIONS: Each question or incomplete statement is followed by several suggested answers or completions. Select the one that BEST answers the question or completes the statement. *PRINT THE LETTER OF THE CORRECT ANSWER IN THE SPACE AT THE RIGHT.*

1. On July 1, 2010, Wardwell, Inc. issued at face value $100,000 in serial bonds with 5% interest payable January 1 and July 1 of each year and principal payable $10,000 on July 1 of each year from 2014 to 2023. Transactions related to this issue decreased working capital during 2015 by
   A. $14,250
   B. $14,500
   C. $4,250
   D. $4,500
   E. none of the above

   1._____

2. With certain of its products, Treat Foods, Inc. includes coupons having no expiration date which are redeemable in merchandise. In the company's experience, 40% of such coupons are redeemed. The liability for unredeemed coupons at December 31, 2013 was $9,000. During 2014, coupons worth $18,000 were issued and merchandise worth $8,000 was distributed in exchange for coupons redeemed. The December 31, 2014 balance sheet should include a liability of
   A. $9,800
   B. $13,000
   C. $8,200
   D. $7,600
   E. none of the above

   2._____

3. A business determines its inventory policy using the economic-order-quantity model that allows a finite stockout cost per period and backordering. Which one of the following statements ACCURATELY describes that stockout cost? The
   A. stockout cost will have to be accumulated in a special account for comparison with expected stockout cost
   B. smaller the stockout cost, the more often stockout will occur
   C. larger the stockout cost, the more often stockout will occur
   D. smaller the stockout cost, the larger will be the average amount of inventory on hand

   3._____

4. The following data refer to various annual costs relating to the inventory of a single-product company:

	Cost Per Unit
Transportation-in on purchases	$.20
Storage	.12
Insurance	.10
	Total Per Year
Interest that could have been earned on alternate investment of funds	$800
Units required	10,000

   4._____

What is the annual carrying cost per unit?
A. $.22   B. $.30   C. $.42   D. $.50

5. A company bought Machine 1 on March 5, 2014 for $5,000 cash. The estimated salvage was $200 and the estimated life was eleven years. On March 5, 2015, the company learned that it could purchase a different machine for $8,000 cash. The new machine would save the company an estimated $250 per year compared to Machine 1. The new machine would have no estimated salvage and an estimated life of ten years. The company could get $3,000 for Machine 1 on March 5, 2015. Ignoring income taxes, which of the following calculations would BEST assist the company in deciding whether to purchase the new machine? (Present value of an annuity of $250)
A. + $3,000 - $8,000
B. - $8,000
C. + $3,000 - $8,000 - $5,000
D. + $3,000 - $8,000 - $4,800

6. A company had income of $50,000 using direct costing for a given period. Beginning and ending inventories for the period were 13,000 units and 18,000 units, respectively. Ignoring income taxes, if the fixed overhead application rate was $2.00 per unit, what was the income using absorption costing?
A. $40,000
B. $50,000
C. $60,000
D. Cannot be determined from the information given

7. The following data apply to Frond Corporation for a given period:

Total variable cost per unit $3.50
Contribution margin sales   30%
Break-even sales (present volume) $1,000,000

Front wants to sell an additional 50,000 units at the same selling price and contribution margin.
By how much can fixed costs increase to generate a gross margin equal to 10% of the sales value of the additional 50,000 units to be sold?
A. $50,000   B. $57,500   C. $67,500   D. $125,000

8. Your client, a retail store, is interested in the relationship between sales (independent variable) and theft losses (dependent variable). Using the proper formula, you compute the coefficient of correlation as .95. What can you definitely conclude about these factors (sales and theft losses)?
A. An increase in sales causes an increase in theft losses.
B. Movement of these factors is in opposite directions.
C. Movement of these factors is entirely unrelated.
D. Movement of these factors is in the same direction.

Questions 9-12.

DIRECTIONS: Questions 9 through 12 are to be answered on the basis of the following information.

The Folding Department foreman must decide each week whether his department will operate normally the following week. He may order a corrective action if he feels the Folding Department will operate inefficiently; otherwise, he does nothing. The foreman receives a weekly Folding Department efficiency-variance report from the Accounting Department. A week in which the Folding Department operates inefficiently is usually preceded by a large efficiency variance. The graph below gives the probability that the Folding Department will operate normally in the following week as a function of the magnitude of the current week's variance reported to the foreman.

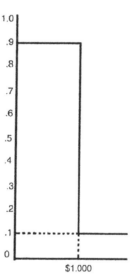

9. An efficiency variance of $1,500 this week means the probability of operating normally the following week is
   A. 0%   B. 10%   C. 90%   D. 100%

10. What are the possible relationships between the current efficiency and next week's operations? Large variance followed by
    A. normal operation, large variance followed by inefficient operation, small variance followed by normal operation, and small variance followed by inefficient operation
    B. normal operation, small variance followed by inefficient operation, and small variance followed by normal operation
    C. inefficient operation, small variance followed by normal operation, and small variance followed by inefficient operation
    D. 90% of normal operation, small variance followed by 10% of normal operation, large variance followed by inefficient operation, and small variance followed by inefficient operation

11. If the foreman can determine for certain whether the Folding Department will operate normally next week, and the cost of corrective action is less than the extra cost of operating the Folding Department inefficiently, then the BEST decision rule for the foreman to follow is:
    A. If normal operations are predicted, do not take corrective action; if inefficient operations are predicted, take corrective action
    B. Regardless of the current variance, do not take corrective action
    C. If normal operations are predicted, take corrective action; if inefficient operations are predicted, do not take corrective action
    D. Regardless of the current variance, take corrective action

12. The following cost information is relevant to the Folding Department foreman in deciding whether corrective action is warranted:
    $500 = cost of corrective action, which will assure normal operation of Folding Department for the following week
    $3,000 = excess cost of operating Folding Department inefficiently for one week
    The foreman receives a report that the Folding Department efficiency variation is $600. The expected cost of NOT taking corrective action is
    A. $0   B. $300   C. $2,700   D. $3,000

13. The calculation of the number of times bond interest is earned involves dividing _____ by annual bond interest expense.
    A. net income
    B. net income plus income taxes
    C. net income plus income taxes and bond interest expense
    D. sinking fund earnings

14. The dating of retained earnings is associated with
    A. earnings accumulated by a subsidiary corporation subsequent to the date of acquisition
    B. earnings accumulated by a foreign subsidiary subsequent to the date of a currency devaluation
    C. the date directors met and declared the corporation was overcapitalized
    D. earnings accumulated subsequent to the date of a quasi-reorganization

15. If a company classifies its expenses as cost of goods sold, employee salaries and benefits, depreciation, taxes, purchased services, and other expenses, the classification basis used is by
    A. area of responsibility   B. object of expenditure
    C. services received   D. function performed

16. Price index numbers generally are used in connection with the
    A. LIFO retail inventory method
    B. annuity method of calculating depreciation
    C. amortization of premium or discount of serial bond issues
    D. calculation of past service costs of pension plans

17. A general description of the depreciation methods applicable to major classes of depreciable assets
    A. is not a current practice in financial reporting
    B. is not essential to a fair presentation of financial position
    C. is needed in financial reporting when company policy differs from income tax policy
    D. should be included in corporate financial statements or notes thereto

18. Gerard Company exchanged 100 shares of treasury stock (its $50 par value common stock) for some land to be used in its business. The treasury stock had cost $60 per share, and, on the exchange date, it had a fair market value of $65 per share. Gerard received $1,200 for scrap when an existing building was immediately removed from this land. Based on these facts, at what amount should this land be capitalized?
    A. $3,800   B. $4,800   C. $5,300   D. $6,500

19. Goldbug Cereals, Inc. distributes coupons to customers which may be presented (on or before a stated expiration date) to grocers for discounts on certain cereals. The grocers are reimbursed when they send the coupons to Goldbug. In the company's experience, 30% of such coupons are redeemed and, on the average, one month elapses between the date a grocer receives a coupon from the buyer and the date Goldbug receives it. On May 1, 2015, Goldbug issues coupons with a total value of $10,000 and an expiration date to the buyer of December 31, 2015. As of December 31, 2015, Goldbug had disbursed $2,500 to grocers for these coupons. The December 31, 2015 balance sheet should include a liability for unredeemed coupons of
    A. $0   B. $375   C. $500   D. $2,250

20. Egale Corporation issued voting preferred stock with a fair value of $1,000,000 in exchange for all of the outstanding common stock of Preye Service Company. Preye has tangible net assets with a book value of $500,000 and a fair value of $600,000. In addition, Egale Corporation issued stock valued at $100,000 to an investment banker as a *finder's fee* for arranging the combination. As a result of this combination, Egale Corporation should record an increase in net assets of
    A. $500   B. $700,000   C. $600,000   D. $1,100,000

6 (#1)

KEY (CORRECT ANSWERS)

1.	A	11.	A
2.	C	12.	B
3.	B	13.	C
4.	B	14.	D
5.	A	15.	B
6.	C	16.	A
7.	A	17.	D
8.	D	18.	C
9.	B	19.	C
10.	A	20.	D

TEST 2

DIRECTIONS: Each question or incomplete statement is followed by several suggested answers or completions. Select the one that BEST answers the question or completes the statement. *PRINT THE LETTER OF THE CORRECT ANSWER IN THE SPACE AT THE RIGHT.*

Questions 1-9.

DIRECTIONS: Questions 1 through 9 are to be answered on the basis of the transactions of Concepcion City.

1. In preparing the general-fund budget of Concepcion City for the forthcoming fiscal year, the city council appropriated a sum greater than expected revenues. This action of the council will result in a(n)
   A. cash overdraft during that fiscal year
   B. increase in encumbrances by the end of that fiscal year
   C. decrease in the fund balance
   D. necessity for compensatory offsetting action in the debt-service fund

   1.____

2. Concepcion City's water utility, which is an enterprise fund, submits a bill for $9,000 to the general fund for water service supplied to city departments and agencies. Submission of this bill would result in
   A. creation of balances which will be eliminated on the city's combined balance sheet
   B. recognition of revenue by the water-utility fund and of an expenditure by the general fund
   C. recognition of an encumbrance by both the water-utility fund and the general fund
   D. creation of a balance which will be eliminated on the city's combined statement of changes in fund balances

   2.____

3. Concepcion City's water utility, which is an enterprise fund, transferred land and a building to the general city administration for public use at no charge to the city. The land was carried on the water-utility books at $4,000 and the building at a cost of $30,000, on which $23,000 depreciation had been recorded. In the year of the transfer, what would be the effect of the transaction?
   A. Reduce retained earnings of the water utility by $11,000 and increase the fund balance of the general fund by $11,000
   B. Reduce retained earnings of the water utility by $11,000 and increase the total assets in the general fixed-assets group by $11,000
   C. Reduce retained earnings of the water utility by $11,000 and increase the total assets in the general fixed-assets group by $34,000
   D. Have no effect on a combined balance sheet for the city

   3.____

4. Concepcion City has approved a special-assessment project in accordance with applicable laws. Total assessments of $500,000, including 10% for the city's share of the cost, have been levied. The levy will be collected from property owners in ten equal annual installments commencing with the current year. Recognition of the approval and levy will result in entries of _____ in the special-assessment fund and _____ in the general fund.
   A. $500,000; $50,000
   B. $450,000; $50,000
   C. $50,000; $50,000
   D. $50,000; no entry

5. What would be the effect on the general-fund balance in the current fiscal year of recording a $15,000 purchase for a new fire truck out of general fund resources, for which a $14,600 encumbrance had been recorded in the general fund in the previous fiscal year?
   A. Reduce the general-fund balance $15,000
   B. Reduce the general-fund balance $14,600
   C. Reduce the general-fund balance $400
   D. Have no effect on the general-fund balance

6. Concepcion City's debt-service fund (for term bonds) recorded required additions and required earnings for the current fiscal year of $15,000 and $7,000, respectively. The actual revenues and interest earnings were $16,000 and $6,500, respectively. What are the necessary entries to record the year's actual additions and earnings in the debt-service fund and in the general long-term debt group, respectively?
   A. $22,500 and $22,000
   B. $22,000 and $22,000
   C. $22,500 and $22,500
   D. $22,500 and no entry

7. Concepcion City serves as collecting agency for the local independent school district and for a local water district. For this purpose, Concepcion City has created a single-agency fund and charges the other entities a fee of 1% of the gross amount collected. (The service fee is treated as general-fund revenue.) During the latest fiscal year, a gross amount of $268,000 was collected for the independent school district and $80,000 for the water district. As a consequence of the foregoing, Concepcion's general fund should
   A. recognize receipts of $348,000
   B. recognize receipts of $344,520
   C. record revenue of $3,480
   D. record encumbrances of $344,520

8. When Concepcion City realized $1,020,000 from the sale of a $1,000,000 bond issue, the entry in its capital-project fund was

Cash	$1,020,000	
Revenues		$1,000,000
Premium on bonds		20,000

   Recording the transaction in this manner indicates that
   A. the $20,000 cannot be used for the designated purpose of the fund but must be transferred to another fund
   B. the full $1,020,000 can be used by the capital-project fund to accomplish its purpose

3 (#2)

C. the nominal rate of interest on the bonds is below the market rate for bonds of such term and risk
D. a safety factor is being set aside to cover possible contract defaults on the construction

9. What will be the balance sheet effect of recording $50,000 of depreciation in the accounts of a utility, an enterprise fund owned by Concepcion City? 9._____
   A. Reduce total assets of the utility fund and the general fixed-assets group by $50,000
   B. Reduce total assets of the utility fund by $50,000 but have no effect on the general fixed-assets group
   C. Reduce total assets of the general fixed-assets group by $50,000 but have no effect on assets of the utility fund
   D. Have no effect on total assets of either the utility fund or the general fixed-assets group

Questions 10-14.

DIRECTIONS: Questions 10 through 14 are to be answered on the basis of the following information.

The Foge Company marks up all merchandise at 25% of gross purchase price. All purchases are made on account with terms of 1/10, net/60. Purchase discounts, which are recorded as miscellaneous income, are always taken. Normally, 60% of each month's purchases are paid for in the month of the purchase while the other 40% are paid during the first ten days of the first month after purchase. Inventories of merchandise at the end of each month are kept at 30% of the next month's projected cost of goods sold.

Terms for sales on account are 2/10, net/30. Cash sales are not subject to discount. Fifty percent of each month's sales on account are collected during the month of the sale, 45% are collected in the succeeding month, and the remainder are usually uncollectible. Seventy percent of the collections in the month of sale are subject to discount while 10% of the collections in the succeeding month are subject to discount.

Projected sales data for selected months follow:

	Sales on Account-Gross	Cash Sales
December	$1,900,000	$400,000
January	1,500,000	250,000
February	1,700,000	350,000
March	1,600,000	300,000

10. Projected gross purchases for January are 10._____
    A. $1,400,000 B. $1,470,000 C. $1,472,000
    D. $1,248,000 E. none of the above

11. Projected inventory at the end of December is 11._____
    A. $420,000 B. $441,600 C. $552,000
    D. $393,750 E. none of the above

12. Projected payments to suppliers during February are
    A. $1,551,200 B. $1,535,688 C. $1,528,560
    D. $1,509,552 E. none of the above

13. Projected sales discounts to be taken by customers making remittances during February are
    A. $5,250 B. $15,925 C. $30,500
    D. $11,900 E. none of the above

14. Projected total collections from customers during February are
    A. $1,875,000 B. $1,861,750 C. $1,511,750
    D. $1,188,100 E. none of the above

15. For bonds payable with a term of 20 years, originally issued at a discount and outstanding for 10 years, the theoretically preferred presentation in the statement of financial position is the
    A. amount expected to be paid to the bondholders at bond maturity date less the present value of interest to be paid in future periods
    B. face amount of the bonds less the discount at the date of issue
    C. bond maturity value less the unamortized discount when the compound-interest method of amortization is used
    D. face amount of the bonds

16. Callan Company exchanged inventory items that cost $8,000 and normally sold for $12,000 for a new delivery truck with a list price of $13,000. The delivery truck should be recorded on Callan's books at
    A. $8,000 B. $8,667 C. $12,000 D. $13,000

17. Bona Facta Company received $20,000 in cash and a used computer with a fair value of $180,000 from Sunbody Corporation for Bona Facta's existing computer having a fair value of $200,000 and an undepreciated cost of $160,000 recorded on its books. How much gain should Bona Facta recognize on this exchange and at what amount should the acquired computer be recorded, respectively?
    A. Zero and $140,000
    B. $4,000 and $144,000
    C. $20,000 and $160,000
    D. $40,000 and $180,000

18. Four G Co., a specialty clothing store, uses the retail-inventory method. The following information relates to 2015 operations:

Inventory January 1, 2015, at cost	$14,200
Inventory January 1, 2015, at sales price	20,100
Purchases in 2015 at cost	32,600
Purchases in 2015 at sales price	50,000
Additional mark-ups on normal sales price	1,900
Sales (including $4,200 on items, which were marked down from $6,400)	60,000

    The cost of the December 31, 2015 inventory determined by the retail-inventory method is
    A. $9,800 B. $6,370 C. $6,743 D. $6,543

5 (#2)

19. On January 1, 2015, Raoul Co. signed a ten-year non-cancellable lease for certain machinery. The terms of the lease call for payments of $10,000 per year to be made by Raoul for ten years. The machinery has a twenty-year life and no salvage value. Raoul uses the straight-line depreciation method on all depreciable assets. Assume that, in substance, this lease is an installment purchased of the machinery by Raoul, and, accordingly, should be capitalized. Assuming a 10% discount rate, the lease payments have a present value of $61,440. Relative to the capitalized lease described above, Raoul's 2015 income statement should include interest expense of
   A. $10,000 and depreciation expense of $3,072
   B. $10,000 only
   C. $6,144 and depreciation expense of $3,072
   D. $6,928 and depreciation expense of $3,072

19._____

20. On July 1, 2015, Wild Bill Co. granted William Hickox, an employee, an option to buy 100 shares of Wild Bill Co. stock for $20 per share, the option exercisable for five years from date of grant. Hickox exercised his option on September 1, 2015, and sold his 100 shares on December 1, 2015. Quoted market prices of Wild Bill Co. stock during 2015 were
   July 1 $20 per share
   September 1 $24 per share
   December 1 $27 per share
   As a result of the option granted to Hickox, Wild Bill should recognize compensation expense on its books in the amount of
   A. $0   B. $300   C. $400   D. $700

20._____

KEY (CORRECT ANSWERS)

1.	C	11.	A
2.	B	12.	B
3.	B	13.	E
4.	A	14.	B
5.	C	15.	C
6.	C	16.	C
7.	C	17.	B
8.	A	18.	B
9.	B	19.	C
10.	C	20.	A

EXAMINATION SECTION

TEST 1

DIRECTIONS: Each question or incomplete statement is followed by several suggested answers or completions. Select the one that BEST answers the question or completes the statement. *PRINT THE LETTER OF THE CORRECT ANSWER IN THE SPACE AT THE RIGHT.*

1. Which of the following is a required disclosure in the earnings statement when reporting the disposal of a segment of the business?
   A. The gain or loss on disposal should be reported as an extraordinary item.
   B. Results of operations of a discontinued segment should be disclosed immediately below extraordinary items.
   C. Earnings per share from both continuing operations and net earnings should be disclosed on the face of the earnings statement.
   D. Revenue and expenses applicable to the discontinued operations should be disclosed in the earnings statement.

   1.____

2. How should research and development costs be accounted for, according to standard accounting practice?
   A. Must be capitalized when incurred and then amortized over their estimated useful lives.
   B. Must be expensed in the period incurred unless contractually reimbursable.
   C. May be either capitalized or expensed when incurred, depending upon the facts of the situation.
   D. May be expensed in the period incurred unless it can be clearly demonstrated that the expenditure will have significant future benefits.

   2.____

Questions 3-5.

DIRECTIONS: Questions 3 through 5 are to be answered on the basis of the following information.

On January 1, 2015, Latham Co. sold machinery on the following terms: The buyer signed a noninterest-bearing note obligating him to pay $1,000 per year for ten years, the first payment to be made on December 31, 2015. Had the buyer tried to arrange for financing of the purchase through an independent financing institution, a 10% rate of interest would have been charged. In this situation, standard accounting practice requires that interest be imputed for financial reporting purposes.
   Assume that, for income tax purposes, interest must also be imputed, but at a 5% rate. Latham's income tax rate is 50%.
   The following are taken from tables of present values:
   Present Value of $1 for 10 Periods
   5% per period $0.6139
   10% per period $0.3855

Present Value of an Annuity of 1 Per Period for 10 Periods
5% per period $7.7217
10% per period $6.1446

3. The amount which should be recorded by Latham for financial reporting purposes as a discount on the note receivable at January 1, 2015 is (rounded to the nearest dollar)
   A. $6,145   B. $3,855   C. $2,278   D. $1,577

4. The amount which should be recorded by Latham on January 1, 2015 as deferred income taxes relative to the sale of the machinery is
   A. $1,928   B. $789   C. $1,139   D. $0

5. In 2015, Latham should recognize interest income on the note of
   A. $386   B. $1,000   C. $614   D. $772

Questions 6-9.

DIRECTIONS: Questions 6 through 9 are to be answered on the basis of the accounts of a large non-profit hospital which properly maintains four funds: operating, special purpose, endowment, and plant.

6. The endowment fund consists of several small endowments, each for a special purpose. The hospital treasurer has determined that it would be legally possible and more efficient to pool the assets and allocate the resultant revenue. The soundest basis on which to allocate revenue after assets are pooled and comply with the special purposes of each endowment would be to
   A. determine market values of securities or other assets comprising each endowment at the time of transfer to the pool and credit revenue to each endowment on that pro rata basis
   B. determine book value of each endowment at the time of transfer to the pool and credit revenue to each endowment on that pro rate basis
   C. apportion future revenue in the moving-average ratio that the various endowments have earned revenue in the past
   D. ask the trustee who administers the pooled assets to make the determination since he is in a position to know which assets are making the greatest combination

7. How should charity service, contractual adjustments, and bad debts be classified in the statement of revenues and expenses for the hospital?
   A. All three should be treated as expenses.
   B. All three should be treated as deductions from patient-service revenues.
   C. Charity service and contractual adjustments should be treated as revenue deductions while bad debts should be treated as an expense.
   D. Charity service and bad debts should be treated as expenses while contractual adjustments should be treated as a revenue deduction.

8. Depreciation on some hospital fixed assets, referred to as *minor equipment*, is not accounted for in the conventional manner. How is depreciation with respect to these assets accounted for?
   A. Ignored on the basis of immateriality
   B. Handled in essentially the same manner as would be the case if the assets were assigned to the activities of a city and were accounted for in its general fund
   C. Determined periodically by inventorying minor equipment and writing the assets down to their value at the inventory date
   D. Recognized only when minor equipment is replaced

8.____

9. To assure the availability of money for improvements, replacement, and expansion of plant, it would be MOST desirable for the hospital to
   A. use accelerated depreciation to provide adequate funds for eventual replacement
   B. use the retirement or replacement system of depreciation to provide adequate funds
   C. sell assets at the earliest opportunity
   D. transfer cash from the operating fund to the plant fund in amounts at least equal to the periodic depreciation charges

9.____

10. A firm is scheduling a long-term research and development project for a recently received government contract. If a stringent time schedule must be met by a limited research staff and the interrelated activities are extensive and complex, what is the MOST appropriate approach for planning and controlling the project?
    A. Cost-volume-earnings analysis
    B. Parametric programming
    C. Program evaluation review technique (PERT)
    D. Queuing-theory analysis

10.____

11. A firm has data relating total production costs to volume for each quarter during the past five years. During this period, production volume has varied substantially, the method of production has been relatively unchanged, and the cost behavior has been complex. What is the MOST appropriate method for estimating future production costs?
    A. Cost-volume-earnings analysis
    B. Cross-sectional analysis
    C. Program evaluation review technique (PERT)
    D. Time-series or trend-regression analysis

11.____

12. Which of the following statements BEST describes a byproduct? A product
    A. that is produced from material that would otherwise be scrap
    B. that has a lower unit selling priced than the main product
    C. created along with the main product whose sales value does not cover its cost of production
    D. that usually produces a small amount of revenue when compared to the main product revenue

12.____

3 (#1)

13. Application rates for factory overhead BEST reflect anticipated fluctuations in sales over a cycle of years when they are computed under the concept of _____ capacity.
    A. maximum
    B. normal
    C. practical
    D. expected-actual

14. What standard cost variance represents the difference between actual factory overhead incurred and budgeted factory overhead based on actual hours worked?
    A. Volume   B. Spending   C. Efficiency   D. Quantity

15. On January 2, 2015, the Gannon Corporation mortgaged one of its properties as collateral for a $1,000,000, 7% five-year loan. During 201, the general price level increased evenly, resulting in a 5 percent rise for the year. In preparing a balance sheet expressing financial position in terms of the general price level at the end of 2015, at what amount should Gannon report its mortgage note payable?
    A. $950,000   B. $1,000,000   C. $1,025,000   D. $1,050,000

16. In January 2011, the Cleary Company purchased a patent for a new consumer product for $170,000. At the time of purchase, the patent was valid for seventeen years. Due to the competitive nature of the product, the patent was estimated to have a useful life of ten years. During 2015, the product was removed from the market under governmental order because of the potential health hazard present in the product.
    What amount should Cleary charge to expense during 2015, assuming amortization is recorded at the end of each year?
    A. $10,000   B. $17,000   C. $102,000   D. $130,000

17. The following information is available for the Bunkum Company:

	Amounts in Thousands		
	2013	2014	2015
Charge sales	$ 900	$1,100	$1,000
Cash sales	600	800	700
Total	$1,500	$1,900	$1,700
Accounts receivable (end of year)	$ 170	$230	$220
Allowance for doubtful accounts (end of year)	47	30	56
Accounts written off as uncollectable (during the year)	2	50	4

    Assuming there was no change in the method used for estimating doubtful accounts during 2013-2015, what was the balance in the allowance for doubtful accounts at the beginning of 2015?
    A. $0   B. $22,000   C. $45,000   D. $49,000

18. A company sold bonds on July 1, 2015, with a face value of $100,000 and due in ten years. The stated annual interest rate is 6%, payable semi-annually on June 30 and December 31. These bonds were sold to yield 8%. The present value of $1 for twenty periods at 4% is $0.4563. The present value of $1 in arrears for twenty periods at 4% is $13,5903.
For how much did these bonds sell on July 1, 2015 (rounded to the nearest dollar)?

   A. $86,401   B. $91,542   C. $100,000   D. $127,172

   18.____

19. Fraser Company wants to finance some long-term assets by selling bonds. Management projects the earnings before deducting bond interest expense and income taxes as $1,166,000 per year. Fraser's income tax rate is 40%. Management wants its net earnings after deducting bond interest expense and income taxes to be ten times the bond interest expense.
Assuming the bonds can be sold at face value, what amount should Fraser issue at 8%?

   A. Approximately $560,580   B. Exactly $583,000
   C. Exactly $825,000   D. Exactly $874,500

   19.____

20. Which one of the following transactions would affect a statement of changes in financial position in which funds are defined as cash, but not one in which funds are defined as working capital?

   A. Recording a net loss from operations
   B. Amortizing a premium on bond
   C. Acquiring treasury stock
   D. Paying last year's federal income tax liability

   20.____

KEY (CORRECT ANSWERS)

1.	C	11.	D
2.	B	12.	D
3.	B	13.	B
4.	B	14.	B
5.	C	15.	B
6.	A	16.	C
7.	B	17.	B
8.	C	18.	A
9.	D	19.	C
10.	C	20.	D

TEST 2

DIRECTIONS: Each question or incomplete statement is followed by several suggested answers or completions. Select the one that BEST answers the question or completes the statement. *PRINT THE LETTER OF THE CORRECT ANSWER IN THE SPACE AT THE RIGHT.*

1. Arlen Corporation has developed the following flexible budget formula for annual indirect-labor cost:
   Total Cost = $4,800 + $0.50 per machine hour
   Operating budgets for the current month are based upon 20,000 hours of planned machine time. Indirect labor costs included in this planning budget are
   A. $14,800 B. $10,000 C. $14,400 D. $10,400

   1._____

Questions 2-3.

DIRECTIONS: Questions 2 and 3 are to be answered on the basis of the following information.

Grand Turn Company produces a special gear used in automatic transmissions. Each gear sells for $28, and the company sells approximately 500,000 gears each year. Unit cost data for 2015 are presented below:

		Variable	Fixed
Direct Material	$6.00		
Direct Labor	$5.00		
Other Costs:			
Manufacturing		$2.00	$7.00
Distribution		$4.00	$3.00

2. The unit cost of gears for direct-cost-inventory purposes is
   A. $13 B. $20 C. $17 D. $27

   2._____

3. Grand has received an offer from a foreign manufacturer to purchase 25,000 gears. Domestic sales would be unaffected by this transaction. If the offer is accepted, variable distribution costs will increase $1.50 per gear for insurance, shipping, and import duties. The relevant unit cost to a pricing decision on this offer is
   A. $17.00 B. $14.50 C. $28.50 D. $18.50

   3._____

4. A large publicly held company has developed and registered a trademark during 2015. How should the cost of developing and registering the trademark be accounted for?
   A. Charged to an asset account that should not be amortized
   B. Expensed as incurred
   C. Amortized over 25 years if in accordance with management's evaluation
   D. Amortized over its useful life or 17 years, whichever is shorter

   4._____

5. Property, plant, and equipment are conventionally presented in the balance sheet at
   A. replacement cost less accumulated depreciation
   B. historical cost less salvage value
   C. original cost adjusted for general price-level changes
   D. acquisition cost less depreciated portion thereof

6. Which of the following statements is NOT valid as it applies to inventory costing methods?
   A. If inventory quantities are to be maintained, part of the earnings must be invested (plowed back) in inventories when FIFO is used during a period or rising prices.
   B. LIFO tends to smooth out the net income pattern since it matches current cost of goods sold with current revenue, when inventories remain at constant quantities.
   C. When a firm using the LIFO method fails to maintain its usual inventory position (reduces stock on hand below customary levels), there may be a matching of old costs with current revenue.
   D. The use of FIFO permits some control by management over the amount of net income for a period through controlled purchases, which is not true with LIFO.

Questions 7-8.

DIRECTIONS: Questions 7 and 8 are to be answered on the basis of the following information.

Corporation A purchased the net assets of Corporation B for $80,000. On the date of A's purchase, Corporation B had no long-term investments in marketable securities and $10,000 (book and fair value) of liabilities.
The fair values of Corporation B's assets, when acquired, were:

Current assets	$40,000
Noncurrent assets	60,000
Total	$100,000

7. How should the $10,000 difference between the fair value of the net assets acquired ($90,000) and the cost ($80,000) be accounted for by Corporation A?
   A. The $10,000 difference should be credited to retained earnings.
   B. The non-current assets should be recorded at $50,000.
   C. The current assets should be recorded at $36,000 and the non-current assets should be recorded at $54,000.
   D. A deferred credit of $10,000 should be set up and then amortized to income over a period not to exceed forty years.

8. Assume that Corporation A paid $110,000 for Corporation B's net assets, and that all other information given above remains the same. What is the MINIMUM annual difference between financial accounting income and tax income because of this purchase?
   A. Zero
   B. $500
   C. $2,000
   D. Cannot be determined from the information given

9. Equipment in general governmental service that had been constructed ten years before by a capital-projects fund was sold. The receipts were accounted for as unrestricted revenue. Entries are NECESSARY in the
   A. general fund and capital-projects fund
   B. general fund and general fixed-assets group of accounts
   C. general fund, capital-projects fund, and enterprise fund
   D. general fund, capital-projects fund, and general fixed-assets group of accounts

10. Cash secured from property tax revenue was transferred for the eventual payment of principal and interest on general obligation bonds. The bonds had been issued when land had been acquired several years ago for a city park. Upon the transfer, an entry would NOT be made in which of the following?
    A. Debt-service fund
    B. General fixed-assets group of accounts
    C. General long-term debt group of accounts
    D. General fund

11. Part of the general obligation bond proceeds from a new issuance was used to pay for the cost of a new city hall as soon as construction was completed. The remainder of the proceeds are transferred to repay the debt. Entries are needed to record these transactions in the
    A. general fund and general long-term debt group of accounts
    B. general fund, general long-term debt group of accounts, and debt-service fund
    C. trust fund, debt-service fund, and general fixed-assets group of accounts
    D. general long-term debt group of accounts, debt-service fund, general fixed-assets group of accounts, and capital-projects fund

12. An account for expenditures does NOT appear in which fund?
    A. Capital projects
    B. Enterprise
    C. Special assessment
    D. Special revenue

13. Authority granted by a legislative body to make expenditures and to incur obligations during a fiscal year is the definition of an
    A. appropriation
    B. authorization
    C. encumbrance
    D. expenditure

14. A city should record depreciation as an expense in its
    A. general fund and enterprise fund
    B. intragovernmental service fund and general fixed-assets group of accounts
    C. enterprise fund and intragovernmental service fund
    D. enterprise fund and capital-projects fund

    14.____

15. A statement of changes in financial position is prepared for which fund?
    A. Enterprise
    B. Intragovernmental service
    C. Special assessment
    D. Trust

    15.____

16. In 2008, Mr. Hoover purchased land for $700,000. In 2013 he died, leaving the land to Alex, his son. The land was appraised for $850,000 at the date of death, and that value was accepted for estate tax purposes. In December 2015, the land was appraised at $950,000.
    How should the land be recorded on Alex's personal financial statement of assets and liabilities as of December 31, 2015?
    A. Cost of zero and appraised value of $950,000
    B. Cost of $700,000 and appraised value of $950,000
    C. Cost of $850,000 and appraised value of $950,000
    D. Appraised value of $950,000 only

    16.____

17. On January 16, 2015, Tann, Inc. granted its employees options to purchase 10,000 shares of its common stock. These options were exercisable beginning immediately and ran for three years from the date of the grant. The options were considered as additional employee compensation. Relevant data follow:
    Par value of stock $6 per share
    Market price at January 16, 2015 $9 per share
    Option price $9 per share
    Options exercised May 1, 2015   5,000 shares
    Market price at May 1, 2015 $12 per share
    Tann is a calendar-year company. The remaining options were not exercised during 2015. How much should Tann have recorded in 2015 as compensation expense and deferred compensation, respectively?
    A. Zero for both
    B. $10,000 and $20,000
    C. $15,000 and $15,000
    D. $30,000 and zero

    17.____

18. The Excavator Company acquired a tract of land containing an extractable natural resource. Excavator Company is required by its purchase contract to restore the land to a condition suitable for recreational use after it extracts the natural resource. Geological surveys estimate that recoverable reserves will be 3,000,000 tons, and that the land will have a value of $600,000 after restoration. Relevant cost information follows:
    Land $6,000,000
    Restoration   900,000
    Geological surveys   300,000
    If Excavator Company maintains no inventories of extracted material, what should be the charge to depletion expense per ton of material extracted?
    A. $1.80   B. $1.90   C. $2.00   D. $2.20

    18.____

5 (#2)

Questions 19-20.

DIRECTIONS: Questions 19 and 20 are to be answered on the basis of the following information.

The Whirling Sales Company uses the retail-inventory method to value its merchandise inventory. The following information is available:

	Cost	Retail
Beginning inventory	$ 40,000	$ 70,000
Purchases	290,000	400,000
Freight-in	2,000	-
Markups (net)	-	3,000
Markdowns (net)	-	5,000
Employee discounts	-	1,000
Sales	-	390,000

19. What is the ending inventory at retail? 19.____
    A. $71,000   B. $72,000   C. $77,000   D. $78,000

20. If the ending inventory is to be valued at the lower of cost or market, what is the cost to retail ratio? $332,000 ÷ 20.____
    A. $468,000   B. $472,000   C. $473,000   D. $474,000

KEY (CORRECT ANSWERS)

1.	D		11.	D
2.	A		12.	B
3.	D		13.	A
4.	C		14.	C
5.	D		15.	A
6.	D		16.	C
7.	B		17.	A
8.	B		18.	D
9.	B		19.	C
10.	B		20.	C

ACCOUNTING

EXAMINATION SECTION

TEST 1

DIRECTIONS: Each question or incomplete statement is followed by several suggested answers or completions. Select the one that BEST answers the question or completes the statement. *PRINT THE LETTER OF THE CORRECT ANSWER IN THE SPACE AT THE RIGHT.*

Questions 1-5.

DIRECTIONS: Questions 1 through 5 are to be answered on the basis of the following information.

When balance sheets are analyzed, working capital always receives close attention. Adequate working capital enables a company to carry sufficient inventories, meet current debts, take advantage of cash discounts and extend favorable terms to customers. A company that is deficient in working capital and unable to do these things is in a poor competitive position.

Below is a Trial Balance as of June 30, 2021, in alphabetical order, of the Worth Corporation.

	Debits	Credits
Accounts Payable		$50,000
Accounts Receivable	$40,000	
Accrued Expenses Payable		10,000
Capital Stock		10,000
Cash	20,000	
Depreciation Expense	5,000	
Inventory	60,000	
Plant & Equipment (net)	30,000	
Retained Earnings		20,000
Salary Expense	35,000	
Sales		100,000
	$190,000	$190,000

1. The Worth Corporation's Working Capital, based on the data above, is 1.____
   A. $50,000   B. $55,000   C. $60,000   D. $65,000

2. Which one of the following transactions increases Working Capital? 2.____
   A. Collecting outstanding accounts receivable
   B. Borrowing money from the bank based upon a 90-day interest-bearing note payable
   C. Paying off a 60-day note payable to the bank
   D. Selling merchandise at a profit

3. The Worth Corporation's Current Ratio, based on the above data, is
   A. 1.7 to 1   B. 2 to 1   C. 2.5 to 1   D. 4 to 3

   3.____

4. Which one of the following transactions decreases the Current Ratio?
   A. Collecting an account receivable
   B. Borrowing money from the bank giving a 90-day interest-bearing note payable
   C. Paying off a 60-day note payable to the bank
   D. Selling merchandise at a profit

   4.____

5. The payment of a current liability, such as Payroll Taxes Payable, will
   A. *increase* the current ratio but have no effect on the working capital
   B. *increase* the Working Capital, but have no effect on the current ratio
   C. *decrease* both the current ratio and working capital
   D. *increase* both the current ratio and working capital

   5.____

6. During the year 2021, the Ramp Equipment Co. made sales to customers totaling $100,000 that were subject to sales taxes of $8,000. Net cash collections totaled $92,000. Discounts of $3,000 were allowed. During the year 2021, uncollectible accounts in the sum of $2,000 were written off the books.
   The net change in accounts receivable during the year 2021 was
   A. $10,500   B. $11,000   C. $13,000   D. $13,500

   6.____

7. The Grable Co. received a $6,000, 8%, 60-day note dated May 1, 2021 from a customer. On May 16, 2021, the Grable Co. discounted the note at 6% at the bank.
   The net proceeds from the discounting of the note amounted to
   A. $5,954.40   B. $6,034.40   C. $6,064.80   D. $6,080.00

   7.____

8. In reviewing the customers' accounts in the Accounts Receivable Ledger for the entire year 2020, the following errors are discovered.
   - A sale in the amount of $500 to the J. Brown Co. was erroneously posted to the K. Brown Co.
   - A sales return of $100 from the Gale Co. was debited to their account.
   - A check was received from a customer, M. White and Co. in payment of a sale of $500 less 2% discount. The check was entered properly in the cash receipts book but was posted to the M. White and Co. account in the amount of $490.

   The difference between the controlling account and its related accounts receivable schedule amounts to
   A. $90   B. $110   C. $190   D. $210

   8.____

9. Assume that you are called upon to audit a cash fund. You find in the cash drawer postage stamps and I.O.U.'s signed by employees, totaling together $425.
   In preparing a financial report, the $425 should be reported as
   A. petty cash   B. investments
   C. supplies and receivables   D. cash

   9.____

10. On December 31, 2020, before adjustment, Accounts Receivable had a debit balance of $60,000 and the Allowance for Uncollectible Accounts had a debit balance of $1,000.
If credit losses are estimated at 5% of Accounts Receivable and the estimated method of reporting bad debts is used, then bad debts expense for the year 2020 would be reported as
   A. $1,000   B. $2,000   C. $3,000   D. $4,000

10.____

Questions 11-12.

DIRECTIONS: Questions 11 and 12 are to be answered on the basis of the following information.

Accrued salaries payable on $7,500 had not been recorded on December 31, 2021. Office supplies on hand of $2,500 at December 32, 2021 were erroneously treated as expense instead of inventory. Neither of these errors was discovered or corrected.

11. These two errors would cause the income for 4021 to be
   A. *understated* by $5,000
   B. *overstated* by $5,000
   C. *understated* by $10,000
   D. *overstated* by $10,000

11.____

12. The effect of these errors on the retained earnings at December 31, 2021 would be
   A. *understated* by $2,500
   B. *overstated* by $2,500
   C. *understated* by $5,000
   D. *overstated* by $5,000

12.____

Questions 13-14.

DIRECTIONS: Questions 13 and 14 are to be answered on the basis of the following information.

Albano, Borrone, and Colluci operate a retail store under the trade name of ABC. Their partnership agreement provides for equaling sharing profits and losses after salaries of $5,000 to Albano, $10,000 to Borrone, and $15,000 to Colluci.

13. If the net income of the partnership (prior to salaries to partners) is $21,000, then Albano's share of the profits, considering all aspects of the agreement, is determined to be
   A. $2,000   B. $3,000   C. $5,000   D. $7,000

13.____

14. The share of the profits that apply to Borrone, similarly, is determined to be
   A. $2,000   B. $3,000   C. $5,000   D. $7,000

14.____

Questions 15-17.

DIRECTIONS: Questions 15 through 17 are to be answered on the basis of the following information.

4 (#1)

The Kay Company currently uses FIFO for inventory valuation. Their records for the year ended June 30, 2021 reflect the following:

July 1, 2021 inventory	100,000 units @ 7.50
Purchases during year	400,000 units @ $8.00
Sales during year	350,000 units @ $15.00
Expenses exclusive of income taxes	$1,290,000
Cash balance on June 30, 2021	$250,000
Income tax rate	34%

Assume the July 1, 2021 inventory will be the LIFO Base Inventory.

15. If the company should change to the LIFO as of June 30, 2021, then their income before taxes for the year-ended June 30, 2021, as compared with the income FIFO method, will be
    A. *increased* by $50,000
    B. *decreased* by $50,000
    C. *increased* by $100,000
    D. *decreased* by $100,000

15.____

16. Assuming the given tax rate (45%), the use of the LIFO method will result in an approximate tax expense for fiscal 2021 of
    A. $45,000
    B. $50,000
    C. $72,000
    D. $94,500

16.____

17. Assuming the given tax rate (45%), the use of the LIFO inventory method compared with the FIFO method, will result in a change in the approximate income tax expense for fiscal year 2021 as follows:
    A. *Increase* of $22,500
    B. *Decrease* of $22,500
    C. *Increase* of $45,000
    D. *Decrease* of $45,000

17.____

18. An accountant in an agency, in addition to his regular duties, has been assigned to train a newly appointed assistant accountant. The latter believes that he is not being given the training that he needs in order to perform his duties. Accordingly, the MOST appropriate FIRST step for the assistant accountant to take in order to secure the needed training is to
    A. register for the appropriate courses at the local college as soon as possible
    B. advise the accountant in a formal memo that his apparent lack of interest in the training is impeding his progress
    C. discuss the matter with the accountant privately and try to discover what seems to be the problem
    D. secure such training informally from more sympathetic accountants in the agency

18.____

19. You have worked very hard and successfully helped complete a difficult audit of a large corporation doing business with your agency. Your supervisor gives you a brief nod of approval when you expected a more substantial degree of recognition. You are angry and feel unappreciated.

19.____

Of the following, the MOST appropriate course of action for you to take would be to
A. voice your displeasure to your fellow workers at being taken for granted by an unappreciative supervisor
B. say nothing now and assume that your supervisor's nod of approval may be his customary acknowledgment of efforts well done
C. let your supervisor know that he owes you something by repeatedly stressing the outstanding job you've done
D. ease off on your work quality and productivity until your efforts are finally appreciated

20. You have been assisting in an audit of the books and records of businesses as a member of a team. The accountant in charge of your group tells you to start preliminary work independently on a new audit. This audit is to take place at the offices of the business. The business officers have been duly notified of the audit date. Upon arrival at their offices, you find that their records and files are in disarray and that their personnel are antagonistic and uncooperative.
Of the following, the MOST desirable action for you to take is to
A. advise the business officers that serious consequences may follow unless immediate cooperation is secured
B. accept whatever may be shown or told you on the grounds that it would be unwise to further antagonize uncooperative personnel
C. inform your supervisor of the situation and request instructions
D. leave immediately and return later in the expectation of encountering a more cooperative attitude

20.____

KEY (CORRECT ANSWERS)

1.	C	11.	C
2.	D	12.	A
3.	B	13.	A
4.	B	14.	D
5.	A	15.	B
6.	B	16.	C
7.	B	17.	B
8.	D	18.	C
9.	C	19.	B
10.	D	20.	C

TEST 2

DIRECTIONS: Each question or incomplete statement is followed by several suggested answers or completions. Select the one that BEST answers the question or completes the statement. *PRINT THE LETTER OF THE CORRECT ANSWER IN THE SPACE AT THE RIGHT.*

Questions 1-3.

DIRECTIONS: Questions 1 through 3 are to be answered on the basis of the following information.

The city is planning to borrow money with a 5-year, 7% bond issue totaling $10,000,000 on principle when other municipal issues are paying 8%.
Present value of $1 – 8% - 5 years -68057
Present value of annual interest payments – annuity 8% - 5 years – 3.99271

1. The funds obtained from this bond issue (ignoring any costs relating to issuance) would be, approximately,
   A. $9,515,390   B. $10,000,000   C. $10,484,620   D. $10,800,000

2. At the date of maturity, the bonds will be redeemed at
   A. $9,515,390   B. $10,000,000   C. $10,484,610   D. $10,800,000

3. As a result of this issue, the ACTUAL interest costs each year as related to the 7% interest payments will
   A. be the same as paid ($700,000)
   B. be more than $700,000
   C. be less than $700,000
   D. fluctuate depending on the market conditions

4. Following the usual governmental accounting concepts, the activities of a municipal employee retirement plan, which is financed by equal employer and employee contributions, should be accounted for in a(n)
   A. agency fund   B. intragovernmental service fund
   C. special assessment fund   D. trust fund

Questions 5-7.

DIRECTIONS: Questions 5 through 7 are to be answered on the basis of the following information.

The Balance Sheet of the JLA Corp. is as follows:

Current Assets	$50,000	Current Liabilities	$20,000
Other Assets	75,000	Common Stock	75,000
Total	$125,000	Retained Earnings	30,000
		Total	$125,000

5. The working capital of the JLA Corp. is
   A. $30,000   B. $50,000   C. $105,000   D. $125,000

6. The operating ratio of the JLA Corp. is
   A. 2 to 1   B. 2½ to 1   C. 1 to 2   D. 1 to 2½

7. The stockholders' equity is
   A. $30,000   B. $75,000   C. $105,000   D. $125,000

8. This question is based on the following figures taken from a set of books for the year ending June 30, 2021.

	Trial Balance Before Adjustments	Trial Balance After Adjustments
Commissions Payable	cr...	cr $1,550
Office Salaries	dr $9,500	dr $10,680
Rental Income	cr $4,300	cr $4,900
Accumulated Depreciation	cr $7,000	cr $9,700
Supplies Expense	dr $1,760	dr $1,200

   As a result of the adjustments reflected in the adjusted trial balance, the net income of the company before taxes will be
   A. *increased* by $4,270   B. *decreased* by $4,270
   C. *increased* by $5,430   D. *decreased* by $5,430

9. This question is based on the following facts concerning the operations of a manufacturer of office desks.

Jan. 1, 2021	Goods in Process Inventory	4,260 units	40% complete
Dec. 31, 2021	Goods in Process Inventory	3,776 units	25% complete
Jan. 1, 2021	Finished Goods Inventory	2,630 units	
Dec. 31, 2021	Finished Goods Inventory	3,180 units	

   Sales consummated during the year: 127,460 units

   Assuming that all the desks are the same style, the number of equivalent complete units, manufactured during the year 2021 is
   A. 127,250   B. 127,460   C. 128,010   D. 131,510

Questions 10-11.

DIRECTIONS: Questions 10 and 11 are to be answered on the basis of the following information.

On January 1, 2021, the Lenox Corporation was organized with a cash investment of $50,000 by the shareholders. Some of the corporate records were destroyed. However, you were able to discover the following facts from various sources.

3 (#2)

Accounts Payable at December 31, 2021 (arising from merchandise purchased)	$16,000
Accounts Receivable at December 31, 2021 (arising from the sales of merchandise)	$18,000
Sales for the calendar year 2021	$94,000
Inventory, December 31, 2021	20,000
Cost of Goods Sold is 60% of the selling price	
Bank loan outstanding – December 31, 2021	15,000
Expenses paid in cash during the year	35,000
Expenses incurred but unpaid as of December 31, 2021	4,000
Dividend paid	25,000

10. The CORRECT cash balance is   10.____
    A. $5,600   B. $20,600   C. $38,600   D. $40,600

11. The stockholders' equity on December 31, 2021 is   11.____
    A. $23,600   B. Deficit of $26,400
    C. $27,600   D. $42,400

Questions 12-13.

DIRECTIONS: Questions 12 and 13 are to be answered on the basis of the following facts developed from the records of a company that sells its merchandise on the installment plan.

Sales	Calendar Year 2020	Calendar Year 2021
Total volume of sales	$80,000	$100,000
Cost of Goods Sold	60,000	40,000
Gross Profit	$20,000	$60,000
Cash Collections		
From 2020 Sales	$18,000	$36,000
From 2021 Sales		22,000
Total Cash Collections	$18,000	$58,000

12. Using the deferred profit method of determining thee income from installment   12.____
    sales, the gross profit on sales for the calendar year 2020 was
    A. $4,500   B. $18,000   C. $20,000   D. None

13. Using the deferred profit method of determining the income from installment   13.____
    sales, the gross profit on sales for the calendar year 2021 was
    A. $22,000   B. $22,200   C. $60,000   D. None

Questions 14-15.

DIRECTIONS: Questions 14 and 15 are to be answered on the basis of the data developed from an examination of the records of Ralston, Inc. for the month of April 2021.

4 (#2)

Beginning Inventory: 10,000 units @ $4.00 each

	Purchases			Sales
April 10	20,000 units @ $5 each	April 13	15,000 units @ $8 each
17	60,000 units @ $6 each	21	50,000 units @ $9 each
26	40,000 units @ $7 each	27	50,000 units @ $10 each

14. The gross profit on sales for the month of April, 2021, assuming that inventory is priced on the FIFO basis, is
    A. $330,000   B. $355,000   C. $395,000   D. $435,000   14.____

15. The gross profit on sales for the month of April 2021, assuming that inventory is priced on the LIFO basis is
    A. $330,000   B. $355,000   C. $395,000   D. $435,000   15.____

16. This question is to be answered on the basis of the data presented for June 30, 2021.   16.____

Balance per Bank Statement	$24,019.00
Balance per General Ledger	20,592.64
Proceeds of note collected by the bank which had not been recorded in the Cash account	4,000.00
Interest on note collected by the bank (no book entries made0	39.40
Debit memo for Bank charges for the month of May	23.50
Deposit in Transit (June 30, 2021)	2,144.00
Customer's check returned by the bank due to lack of funds	150.00
Outstanding checks – June 30, 2021	1,631.46
Error in recording check made by our bookkeeper – check cleared in the amount of $463.00 but entered in the bank book for $436.00	

    If we wish to reconcile the bank and book balance so that the bank balance and the book balance are reconciled to a corrected balance, the corrected balance should be
    A. $20,592.64   B. $24,019.00   C. $24,531.54   D. $26,163.00

17. The Ateb Company has issued a $500,000 bond issue on January 2, 2021 at 8% interest, payable semi-annually, sold at par, with interest payable on June 30 and December 31.   17.____
    On September 30, 2021, at the close of the fiscal year of the Ateb Company, the interest expense accrual should reflect interest payable of, approximately,
    A. $10,000   B. $20,000   C. $40,000   D. $50,000

18. Assume that a new procedure requires that a particular and unvarying sequence of steps be followed in order to yield the desired data. You are assigned to be in charge of subordinates working with this procedure.   18.____

Which one of the following is MOST likely to impress subordinates with the importance of following the sequence of steps exactly as given?
A. Explain the consequences of error if the procedure is not followed.
B. Suggest how rewarding would be the feeling of finding errors before the supervisor catches them.
C. Indicate that independent verification of their work will be done by other staff members
D. Advise that upward career mobility usually results from following instructions exactly

19. It is essential for an experienced accountant to know approximately how long it will take him to complete a particular assignment because
A. his supervisors will need to obtain this information only from someone planning to perform the assignment
B. he must arrange his schedule to insure proper completion of the assignment consistent with agency objectives
C. he must measure whether he is keeping pace with others performing similar assignments
D. he must determine what assignments are essential and have the greatest priority within his agency

19._____

20. There are circumstances which call for special and emergency efforts by employees. You must assign your staff to make this type of effort.
Of the following, this special type of assignment is MOST likely to succeed if the
A. time schedule required to complete the assignment is precisely stated but is not adhered to
B. employees are individually free to determine the work schedule
C. assignment is clearly defined
D. employees are individually free to use any procedure or method available to them

20._____

KEY (CORRECT ANSWERS)

1.	A	11.	A
2.	B	12.	A
3.	B	13.	B
4.	D	14.	C
5.	A	15.	B
6.	B	16.	C
7.	C	17.	A
8.	B	18.	A
9.	A	19.	B
10.	B	20.	C

EXAMINATION SECTION
TEST 1

DIRECTIONS: Each question or incomplete statement is followed by several suggested answers or completions. Select the one that BEST answers the question or completes the statement. *PRINT THE LETTER OF THE CORRECT ANSWER IN THE SPACE AT THE RIGHT.*

1. With regard to the requirement of the auditing standard that sufficient and competent evidential matter be obtained, the term competent PRIMARILY refers to the evidence.
   A. consistency
   B. relevance
   C. measurability
   D. dependability

   1._____

2. Audit working papers should NOT
   A. include any client-prepared papers or documents other than those prepared by the auditor
   B. be kept by the auditor after review and completion of the audit except for items required for the income tax return
   C. be submitted to the client to support the financial statements and to provide evidence of the audit work performed
   D. by themselves be expected to provide sufficient support for the auditor's operation

   2._____

3. Mr. Jason Stone operates a small drugstore as an individual proprietor. During the past year, his books were not properly kept. He asks you, as a CPA, to give him some advice concerning the earnings of his business during the calendar year 2011. A review of his bank accounts and a diary of financial data reveal the information presented below:

   Deposits made during 2018 per bank statements totaled $226,000. Deposits include investments made by Mr. Shea as well as a loan he obtained from the bank for $25,000.
   Disbursements during 2018 per bank statement totaled $185,000. Included are personal withdrawals of $15,000 and payments on debt of $10,000.
   Net equity of Jason Stone at January 1, 2018 was determined to be $45,000.
   Net equity of Jason Stone at December 31, 2018 was determined to be $75,000.
   During 2018, funds invested by Jason Stone in the business amounted to $6,500.
   Based upon the *net worth* method, net income for the year ended December, 2018 was
   A. $35,000   B. $38,500   C. $40,000   D. $42,000

   3._____

4. Because of past association, a senior accountant is convinced of the competence and honesty of those who prepared the financial information which he is auditing. He consequently concludes that certain verification procedures are unnecessary. This conclusion by the senior accountant is ill-advised for the proper performance of his present audit MAINLY because the
   A. members of the staff often lack the specialized skills and training without which verification in an audit cannot proceed
   B. verification procedures depend upon the materiality of the subject matter under examination and not upon the personal characteristics of the individuals involved
   C. nature of opinion expressed in the report issued by the senior accountant, at the end of his audit, is grounded on personal considerations
   D. quality of the senior accountant's independence and his objective examination of the information under review is impaired

   4._____

5. Of the following statement ratios, the one that represents *a growth ratio is* 5._____
   A. working capital ratio
   B. acid-test ratio
   C. long-term debt to total capitalization
   D. dollar earnings per share

Questions-6-8.

DIRECTIONS: Questions 6 through 8 are to be answered on the basis of the information given below.
During the course of an examinations of the financial statements of a wholesale establishment, the following facts were revealed for the year ended December 3, 2018:

I. Although merchandise: inventory costing $3,000 was on hand and.was-included in the inventory count on December 31, 2018, title had passed and it was billed to the customer on December 31, 2018 at a sale price of $4,500.
II. Merchandise had been billed to the customer on December 31, 2018 in the amount of $5,200 but had not been shipped to him. This merchandise which cost $3,500, was not included in the inventory at the end of the year. The goods were shipped and title passed on January 15, 2019.
III. Merchandise costing $6,000 was recorded as a purchase on December 31, 2018 but was Not included in the inventory at that date.
IV. Merchandise costing $5,000 was received on January 3, 2019, but was recorded on the books as of December 31, 2018, and included in inventory as of December 31, 2018. The goods were shipped on December 30, 2018 by the vendor F.O.B. shipping point.
V. An examination of receiving records indicated that merchandise costing $7,000 was received on December 31, 2018. It was included in inventory as of that date but not recorded as a purchase.

6. Adjustments to correct the inventory figure will reflect a net adjustment so as to 6._____
   A. reduce it by $6,500   B. increase it by $6,500
   C. reduce it by $8,000   D. increase it by $8,000

7. Adjustments to correct the sales figure will result in a net adjustment to sales of a (n) 7._____
   A. increase by $5,200   B. decrease by $5,200
   C. increase by $6,300   D. decrease by $6,300

8. The net adjustment to purchases for the period ending December 31, 2018 will result in a(n) 8._____
   A. increase of $4,000   B. decrease of $7,000
   C. increase of $7,000   D. decrease of $4,000

Questions 9-10.

DIRECTIONS: Questions 9 and 10 are to be answered on the basis of the information given below.
A company worth $500,000 of common capital stock, par value $100 per share with retained earnings of $100,000, decides to change its capitalization from a par to a no-par basis. It, therefore, called in its 5,000 shares of par value stock and issued in place thereof 10,000 shares of no-par value stock.

9. The balance in the capital stock account after the change is 9._____
   A. $1,000,000   B. $500,000
   C. $,400,000   D. $200,000

10. The balance in the retained earnings account after the change is 10._____
    A. $90,000   B. $100,000   C. $125,000   D. $250,000

11. Among the assets on the December 31, 2018 balance sheet of the Wolf Corporation 11._____
    was the following:
    Investment in Sheep Company
    1,000 shares @ $90 bought January 1, 2018 $90,000
    The net worth section of the balance sheet of the Sheep Company on the same date
    was as follows:

    NET WORTH
    Capital Stock, 1,000 shares $100,000
    Deficit January 1, 2018 $20,000
      Less Operating Profit 2018   15,000
    Deficit December 31, 2018   5,000
    Total Net worth $ 95,000

    The net debit or credit to Consolidated Surplus arising from consolidation of the
    Sheep Company with the parent Wolf Corporation is
    A. $3,000 credit   B. $5,000 credit
    C. $7,000 debit   D. $10,000 credit

Questions 12-15.

DIRECTIONS: Questions 12 through 15 are to be answered on the basis of the
             Trial Balances and the Notes below.

CLIMAX CORPORATION - Trial Balances (000 Omitted)

	December 31, 2018 Debit	December 31, 2018 Credit	December 31, 2017 Debit	December 31, 2017 Credit
Cash	$ 178		$ 84	
Accounts Receivable	300		240	
Allowance for Bad Debts		$ 13		$ 10
Merchandise Inventory	370		400	
Building & Equipment	420		360	
Allowance for Depreciation		180		190
Accounts Payable		220		210
Mortgage Bonds		300		300
Unamortized Bond Discount	18		21	
Capital Stock		357		270
Retained Earnings		125		90
Net Sales		$4,200		$4,000
Cost of Goods Sold	$2,300		$2,100	
Salaries & Wages	1,500		1,400	
Heat & Utilities	110		100	
Depreciation	20		20	
Taxes & Insurance	10		10	
Interest	16		15	
Bad Debts	20		20	
Losso on Equipment Sales (Note 1)	6			
Dividends Paid (Note 2)	127		300	
	$5,395	$5,395	$5,070	$5,070

NOTES: (1) In 2018 equipment costing $40,000 and having a net bookvalue of $10,000 was sold for $4,000.
(2) Dividends paid in 2018 include a stock dividend of $27,000.

12. The net change in working capital from 2017 to 2018 is   12._____
    A. $111,000   B. $130,000   C. $260,000   D. $333,000

13. The amount of funds provided from net income for the year ended December 31, 2018 is   13._____
    A. $214,000   B. $244,000   C. $254,000   D. $284,000

14. The amount of funds applied to dividends during the year 2018 is   14._____
    A. $100,000   B. $125,000   C. $175,000   D. $202,350

15. The amount of funds applied to building and equipment during the year 2018 is   15._____
    A. $100,000   B. $70,000   C. $50,000   D. $30,000

Questions 16-17.

DIRECTIONS: Questions 16 and 17 are to be answered on the basis of the information given below.
The Natural Sales Company issues gift certificates in denominations of $5, $10 and $25. They are redeemable in merchandise having a markup of 30% of Selling Price.

During December, $35,000 of gift certificates was sold and $20,000 was redeemed. It is estimated that 5% of the certificates issued will never be redeemed.

16. The PROPER entry to reflect the current liability with respect to these certificates is   16._____
    A. $13,250   B. $14,250   C. $15,250   D. $16,250

17. The cost of the merchandise issued to meet the redeemed certificates is   17._____
    A. $11,000   B. $13,000   C. $14,000   D. $17,000

Questions 18-19.

DIRECTIONS: Questions 18 and 19 are to be answered on the basis of the information given below.
Arthur Evans commenced business in 2017 but did not maintain a complete set of proper records. He relied on the bank statements in order to compute his income. All his receipts Are deposited, and all his expenditures are made by check.
His bank statements and other records reflected the following:

Bank balance per bank 12/31/2017	$ 14,735
Bank balance per bank 12/31/2018	18,380
Deposits for 2018 per bank statement	209,450
Deposits in transit 12/31/2017	3,590
Deposits in transit 12/31/2018	4,150

Checks returned with the January 2018 bank statement showed a total of $4,770 checks issued in 2018.
2018 checks not returned by the bank at December 31, 2018 amounted to $5,150.
$6,430 of checks were issued in 2018 in payment of purchases made in 2017.
$9,425 of deposits was made by Mr. Evans in 2018 representing 2017 sales.

Unpaid bills for 2018 amounted to $2,150 on December 31, 2018.

Accounts Receivable for 2018 on December 31, 2018 were $10,930.
Merchandise inventory figures on the following dates were:
    December 31, 2017 $13,000
    December 31, 2018   17,580

On July 1, 2018, machinery costing $8,000 was purchased. The estimated life was 5 years with a salvage value of $500.

18. The balance of the cash in the bank according to the books on December 31, 2018 was 18.____
    A. $18,380   B. $17,380   C. $16,380   D. $15,380

19. The Sales Revenue for 2018 was 19.____
    A. $211,515   B. $209,515   C. $208,515   D. $207,515

Questions 20-21.

DIRECTIONS: Questions 20 and 21 are to be answered on the basis of the information given below.

In the examination of an imprest petty cash fund of $600, you were presented with the following fund composition shown below. The date of examining the petty cash fund was the balance sheet date.

Currency - bills	$310.00
Cash - coins	3.15
Postage stamps	50.00
Sales returns memos for cash refunded to customers	15.50
Check of one employee dated one month in advance	75.00
Vouchers for miscellaneous office expenses	100.85
Sales slip of an employee who purchased company merchandise; the money in payment was taken from the fund, entered as cash sale, and the sales slip inserted in the fund	45.50

20. The corrected balance of petty cash for balance sheet purposes is 20.____
    A. $313.15   B. $319.32   C. $347.53   D. $409.27

21. A correcting journal entry to establish the correct fund balance would increase expenses by 21.____
    A. $100.85   B. $212.31   C. $28.28   D. $139.50

22. The PRIMARY objective of an audit, as generally understood in accounting practice, is to 22.____
    A. assert a series of claims for management as to the financial condition of the company
    B. establish the reliability or unreliability as to the financial statements and supporting accounting records of the company
    C. install special procedures involved in the periodic closing of the accounts prior to the preparation of financial statements of the company
    D. summarize accounts and financial transactions to determine the costs of processes or units of production for the company

Questions 23-25.

DIRECTIONS: Questions 23 through 25 are to be answered on the basis of the information given below.

The following data related to the business operations for the calendar years 2016, 2017, and 2018 of the Wholly Corporation.

	2016	2017	2018
Net income per books	$170,000	$190,000	$140,000
Dividends *paid or earned?*	−15,000	20,000	10,000
Purchases made in year 2017 recorded as purchased in 2018 but recorded in inventory in 2017		25,000	
Inventory value December 31, 2018 underestimated			5,000
Depreciation omitted -			
applicable to 2016	− 3,000		
applicable to 2017		− 4,500	
applicable to 2018			6,000
Overstatement of prepaid advertising as of January 1, 2017		− 1,500	
Salaries - earned during 2016 paid during 2017 - no accruals	−18,000		
Payroll taxes on salarie	− 1,440		

23. The net profit for 2016 after adjusting for the facts given above is 23.____
    A. $146,060   B. $150,050   C. $164,200   D. $192,835

24. The net profit for 2017 after adjusting for facts given 24.____
    A. $152,400   B. $165,700   C. $173,145   D. $181,440

25. If the balance of the retained earnings account was $265,000 on January 1, 2016, the balance of the retainedearnings account on December 31, 2018 after corrections is 25.____
    A. $711,500   B. $525,000   C. $424,360   D. $307,420

Questions 26-30.

DIRECTIONS: Each question numbered 26 through 30 consists of a description of a transaction that indicates a two fold change on the balance sheet. Each of these transactions may be classified under one of the following categories. Examine each question carefully. In the correspondingly numbered space at the right, mark the appropriate space for the letter preceding the category below which BEST represents the charges that should be made on the balance sheet, as of December 31, 2017.

A. Current Assets are *overstated* and Retained Earnings are *overstated*
B. Current Assets are *understated* and Retained Earnings are *understated*
C. Current Liabilities are *overstated* and Retained Earnings are *overstated*
D. Current Liabilities are *understated* and Retained Earnings are *overstated*

26. Goods shipped on consignment out were not included in the final inventory although the entries were properly made for such consignments. 26.____

27. A number of cash sales made subsequent to the balance sheet date were recorded as sales in the prior period before the balance sheet date. The merchandise was included in inventories. 27.____

28. A cash dividend declared December 21, 2017, payable on January 15, 2018 to stockholders of record as of December 28, 2017, had not been recorded as of December 31, 2017. 28.____

29. The provision for the allowance for doubtful accounts receivable for the current period that should have been made had not been recorded. 29.____

30. Merchandise received by December 31, 2017, and properly included in inventory on that date, was not entered as a purchase until January 2018. 30.____

Questions 31-33.

DIRECTIONS: Questions 31 through 33 are to be answered on the basis of the information given below.

Ten men work as a group on a particular manufacturing operation. When the weekly production of the group exceeds a standard number of pieces per hour, each man in the group is paid a bonus for the excess production; the bonus is in addition to his wages at the hourly rate. The amount of the bonus is computed by first determining the percentage by which the groups production exceeds the standard. One-half of this percentage is then applied to a wage rate of $1.25 to determine an hourly bonus rate. Each man in the group is paid, as a bonus, the bonus rate applied to his total hours worked during the week. The standard rate of production before a bonus can be earned is two hundred pieces per hour.

The production record for a given week was: Hours Worked Production

Days	Hours worked	Production
Monday	72	17,680
Tuesday	72	17,348
Wednesday	72	18,800
Thuresday	72	18,560
Friday	71.5	17,888
Saturday	40	9,600
	399.5	99,076

31. The rate of the bonus for the week is _____ %. 31.____
    A. 24   B. 20   C. 18   D. 12

32. The bonus paid to the ten-man group for the week is 32.____
    A. $59.93   B. $69.39   C. $95.00   D. $225.00

33. The total wages of one employee who worked 40 hours at a base rate of $1.00 per hour are 33.____
    A. $46   B. $50   C. $54   D. $58

8 (#1)

34. A junior accountant reported to his senior that he had performed the operations listed below.
Which one of the following statements about these operations CORRECTLY describes the operation?
   A. Vouchered the amount of petty cash
   B. Vouchered the receivables ledger accounts with the sales register
   C. Analyzed the fixed assets account
   D. Checked all entries in the general journal to original evidence

34.____

35. Sales during July 2018 for the Major Company were $267,500, of which $170,000 was on account. The sales figure presented to you includes the total sales tax charged to retail customers (assume a sales tax rate of 7%).
The sales tax liability that should be shown at the end of July 2018 is
   A. $8,300   B. $9,400
   C. $17,500   D. $18,750

35.____

Questions 36-37.

DIRECTIONS: Questions 36 and 37 are to be answered on the basis of the information given below.

During the audit of records of the Short Corporation for the year ended December 31, 2018, the auditor was presented with the following information:

The finished goods inventory consisted of 22,000 units carried at a cost of $17,600 at December 31, 2018. The finished goods inventory at the beginning of the year (January 1, 2018) consisted of 24,000 units, priced at a cost of $16,800. During the year, 4,000 units were manufactured at a cost of $3,600 and 6,000 units were sold.

36. To PROPERLY reflect the cost of the finished goods inventory at December 31, 2018, if the FIFO method was used, assuming there was no work-in-process inventory, would require an adjustment of
   A. $1,400 credit   B. $1,400 debit   C. $1,600 credit   D. $1,600 debit

36.____

37. To PROPERLY reflect the cost of the finished goods inventory at December 31, 2018 if the LIFO method was used, assuming there was no work-in-process Inventory, would require an adjustment of
   A. $2,200 debit   B. $2,200 credit   C. $4,200 credit   D. $4,200 debit

37.____

38. Within the general field of auditing, there are internal auditors and independent auditors who differ significantly one from the other in that the latter group:

   A. is responsible for a more complete, detailed examination of accounting data
   B. conduct standard audits established by custom and usage for a particular trade or industry
   C. direct their investigations primarily to matters of fraud and criminal misrepresentation
   D. issue reports for the benefit of other interests, such as shareholders and creditors

38.____

9 (#1)

39. Moreland Corporation sells merchandise at a gross profit of 25% of sales. Fire on the premises of this Corporation on July 16, 2018 resulted in the destruction of the merchandise. The Corporation's merchandise is insured against fire by a $150,000 insurance policy with an 80% co-insurance clause. The Corporation's records show the following:

Sales -- January 1, 2018 to July 16, 2018	$400,000
Inventory -- January 1, 2018	$ 65,000
Purchases -- January 1, 2018 to July 16, 2018	$460,000
Merchandise salvaged	$ 25,000

The amount of inventory destroyed by fire is
A. $150,000   B. $200,000   C. $225,000   D. $300,000

39.____

40. Below are the totals of the cash receipts and disbursement books of the Small Corporation for the calendar year 2018
Receipts $392,369.72
Disbursements $331,477.87
The bank balance on January 1, 2018 was $38,610.21. The bank balance on December 31, 2018 was $101,918.34. No checks were outstanding on January 1, 2018. Checks outstanding on December 31, 2018 amounted to $5,416.28. Undeposited checks on hand December 31, 2018 were $3,000 which are included in the December cash receipts. Bank deposits for the year total $387,643.72.
The total SHORTAGE in cash is
A. $1,726   B. $2,416.28   C. $3,000   D. $3,452

40.____

41. A state corporation, all of whose business is done within the city, showed the following for 2018:

Entire net income	$ 1,000
Salaries to Officers deducted in determining entire net income	$ 40,000
Average capital	$ 450,000

The corporation's city business tax payable (assuming a 7% rate on income and a .001 rate on capital) is
A. $546   B. $450   C. $70   D. $25

41.____

42. Sales revenue serves as the basis for determining _____ taxes.
A. estate   B. excise   C. payroll   D. property.

42.____

43. ABC Corporation operates in the city and would be subjected to the following taxes:
I. Federal Corporation Income Tax – Surtax 26% and Normal Tax 22%
II. State Franchise Tax - 72%
If income before taxes for 2018 was $370,000 per the federal tax return (after establishing estimate), assuming the rates as noted above, the tax liabilities that should be set up are Federal and State.
A. $180,000; $25,800
B. $177,600; $29,700
C. $165,500; $20,000
D. $171,100; $30,000

43.____

44. In the examination of a manufacturing company where inventory values are of a material amount, the client has restricted the extent of the independent CPA's audit examination of his records by not permitting the CPA to observe the taking of inventory at the close of the company's fiscal year. In such a case, which of the following opinions with regard to the audit report would be APPROPRIATE? _____ opinion.
    A. Unqualified
    B. Qualified
    C. Adverse
    D. Disclaimer of

45. Accounting data are subject to error from a variety of sources and for a variety of reasons. Of the following, the MOST efficient way to lessen this problem is to
    A. identify and classify errors as to type and kind as soon as they are detected
    B. provide for machine calculation of accounting data wherever possible
    C. confirm accounting data by independent third parties
    D. designate an individual to be responsible for the accuracy of accounting data

46. Normally, an auditor does NOT rely upon his study and testing of a system of internal control to
    A. evaluate the reliability of the system
    B. uncover embezzlements of the client's system
    C. help determine the scope of other auditing procedures to be followed
    D. gain support for his opinion as to the accuracy and fairness of the financial statements

Questions 47-50.

DIRECTIONS: Questions 47 through 50 are to be answered on the basis of the information given below.

An office clerk who was not familiar with proper accounting procedures prepared the following financial report for the Dunrite Corporation as of June 30, 2018. In addition to the errors in presentation, additional data below were not considered in the preparation of the report. Restate this balance sheet in proper form, giving recognition to the additional data so that you will be able to determine the required information to answer these questions.

DUNRITE CORPORATION
June 30, 2018

CURRENT ASSETS

Cash			$155,000 CA
Marketable securities		81000	82,400 CA
Investment in affiliated company			175,000 LTA
Treasury stock		$ 25,500 EQ	
Less reserve for trea		25,500 EQ	
Accounts receivable		$277,800 CA	
Accounts payable		135,000 CL	142,800
Total current assets			$555,200

PLANT ASSETS

Equipment		$450,000 LTA	
Building	$400,000 LTA		
Reserve for plant expansion	100,000 RE	300,000	
Land		50,000 LTA	
Goodwill		35,000 LTA	
Prepaid expenses		12,000 CA	847,000
Total Assets			$1,402,200

11 (#1)

LIABILITIES
Cash dividend payable $25,000 CL
Stock dividend payable 15,000 EQ
Accrued liabilities 15,700 CL
Bonds payable $400,000 LTL
Sinking fund 325,000 LTL 75,000
Total Current Liabilities $130,700

STOCKHOLDERS' EQUITY
Paid-in capital
  Common stock $550,000 CS   550,000
Retained earnings and reserves
  Premium common stock $74,000 CS
  Reserve - doubtful accounts 7,500 RE
  Reserve - depreciation of equipment 140,000 RE
  Reserve - depreciation building 170,000 RE
  Reserve - income-taxes 50,000 RE CL
  Retained earnings 280,000 RE $721,500
Total Liabilities and Equity $1,402,200

ADDITIONAL DATA:
  A. The reserve for income taxes represents the balance due on the estimated liability for taxes on income of the current fiscal year.
  B. Marketable securities are recorded at cost and have a market value at June 30, 2018 of $81,000. They represent temporary investments.
  C. The investment in the affiliated company is a minority interest carried at cost.
  D. Bonds payable are due 10 years from the balance-sheet date.
  E. The stock dividend payable was declared on June 30, 2018.

47. After restatement of the balance sheet in proper form, and giving recognition to The additional data, the Total Current Assets would be
    A. $509,200   B. $519,700   C. $610,000   D. $735,000   47._____

48. After restatement of the balance sheet in proper form, and giving recognition to the Additional data, the Total Current Liabilities would be
    A. $225,700   B. $325,200   C. $352,700   D. $480,000   48._____

49. After restatement of the balance sheet in proper form, and giving recognition to the additional data, the Stockholders' Equity shows a total of
    A. $730,100   B. $819,000   C. $910,000   D. $1,019,000   49._____

50. After restatement of the balance sheet in proper form, and giving recognition to the additional data, the net book value of the total plant equipment would be
    A. $440,000   B. $590,000   C. $750,000   D. $850,000   50._____

12 (#1)

KEY (CORRECT ANSWERS)

1. D
2. C
3. B
4. D
5. D
6. B
7. B
8. C
9. B
10. B
11. D
12. A
13. B
14. A
15. A
16. A
17. C
18. B
19. A
20. A
21. A
22. B
23. A
24. D
25. A

26. B
27. A
28. D
29. A
30. D
31. D
32. A
33. A
34. C
35. C
36. A
37. B
38. D
39. B
40. A
41. A
42. B
43. D
44. D
45. C
46. B
47. B
48. A
49. D
50. B

TEST 2

DIRECTIONS: Each question or incomplete statement is followed by several suggested answers or completions. Select the one that BEST answers the question or completes the statement. *PRINT THE LETTER OF THE CORRECT ANSWER IN THE SPACE AT THE RIGHT.*

Question 1.

DIRECTIONS: Question 1 is based on the following portion of an income tax withholding table. In answering this question, assume that this table was in effect for the full year.

If the payroll period with respect to an employee is daily:

And the wages are		And the number of witholding exemptions claimed is				
At least	But less than	0	1	2	3	4
		The amount of income tax to be withheld shall be				
$172	$176	$24.40	$20.80	$17.20	$13.60	$10.00
176	180	24.90	21.30	17.70	14.20	10.60
180	184	25.50	18.30	18.30	14.70	11.10

1. K received a daily wage of $176.40 the first 7 pay periods and $182.50 the last 19 pay periods. He claimed 3 exemptions the first 9 pay periods and 4 the rest of the year. Total income tax withheld during the year was
   A. $288.10
   B. $295.30
   C. $316.50
   D. $317.50
   E. none of the above

   1._____

2. A voucher contained the following items:
   6 desks @ 89.20 $525.20
   8 chairs @ 32.50   260.00
                    Total   885.20
   The terms were given on the voucher as 3%, 10 days; net, 30 days. Verify the computations, which may be incorrect, and calculate the correct amount to be paid. If payment is made within the discount period, the amount to be paid is
   A. $761.64
   B. $771.34
   C. $795.20
   D. $858.64
   E. none of the above

   2._____

3. Under the income tax law in effect for last year, an individual who is blind on the last day of the taxable year is entitled to claim an exemption of $600 because of such blindness, in addition to any other exemptions to which he may be entitled.
   Richard Roe, who files his income tax returns on the calendar year basis, became permanently blind on December 15 of last year.
   In filing his income tax return for last year, Mr. Roe may claim an exemption for blindness of
   A. $300
   B. $550
   C. $574
   D. $600
   E. none of the above

   3._____

2 (#2)

4. The Jones Company had a merchandise inventory of $24,625 on January 1 of last year. 4.____
During that year, purchases made by the company amounted to $60,000, sales to $85,065, and cost of goods sold to $28,060.
The inventory on December 31 of last year was
   A. $25,065
   B. $28,500
   C. $49,690
   D. $57,005
   E. none of the above

KEY (CORRECT ANSWERS)

1. D
2. B
3. D
4. E

EXAMINATION SECTION
TEST 1

DIRECTIONS: Each question or incomplete statement is followed by several suggested answers or completions. Select the one that BEST answers the question or completes the statement. *PRINT THE LETTER OF THE CORRECT ANSWER IN THE SPACE AT THE RIGHT.*

1. When a supervisor in a large office introduces a change in the regular office procedure, it is USUAL to expect
    A. immediate acceptance by office staff, unless the change is unnecessary
    B. an immediate production increase, since new procedures are more stimulating than old ones
    C. a temporary production loss, even if the change is really an overall improvement
    D. resistance to the change only if it has been put into writing

    1.____

2. A supervisor evaluates the performance of subordinates and then applies measures, where needed, which result in bringing performance up to desired standards.
   Which of the following functions of management might he BEST be described as performing?
    A. Organizing   B. Controlling   C. Directing   D. Planning

    2.____

3. Assume that, as a supervisor, you have been assigned responsibility for a new and complex project which entails collection and analysis of data. You have prepared general written instructions which explain the project and procedures to be followed by several statisticians.
   Which of the following procedures would be MOST advisable for you, as the supervisor, to follow?
    A. Distribute the instructions to your subordinates to come to you with any important questions
    B. Distribute the instructions and advise subordinates to come to you with any important questions
    C. Meet with subordinates as a group and explain the project using the written instructions as a handout
    D. Delegate responsibility for further explanation of the project to an immediate qualified subordinate to free you for concentration on research design

    3.____

4. Supervisors have an obligation to make careful and thorough appraisals and reports of probationary employees.
   Of the following, the MOST important justification for this statement is that the probationary period
    A. should be used for positive development of the employee's understanding of the organization
    B. is the most effective period for changing a new employee's knowledges, skills, and attitudes

    4.____

C. insures that the employee will meet work standard requirements on future assignments
D. should be considered as the final step in the selection process

5. Many studies of management indicate that a principal reason for failure of supervisors lies in their ability to delegate duties effectively.
Which one of the following practices by a supervisor would NOT be a block to successful delegation?
   A. Instructing the delegate to follow a set procedure in carrying out the assignment
   B. Maintaining point-by-point control over the process delegated
   C. Transferring ultimate responsibility for the duties assigned to the delegate
   D. Requiring the delegate to keep the delegator informed of his progress

6. Crosswise communication occurs between personnel at lower or middle levels of different organizational units. It often speeds information and improves understanding, but has certain dangers.
Of the following proposed policies, which would NOT be important as a safeguard in crosswise communication?
   A. Supervisors should agree as to how crosswise communication should occur.
   B. Crosswise relationships must exist only between employees of equal status.
   C. Subordinates must keep their superiors informed about their interdepartmental communications.
   D. Subordinates must refrain from making commitments beyond their authority.

7. Systems theory has given us certain principles which are as applicable to organizational and social activities as they are to those of science.
With regard to the training of employees in an organization, which of the following is likely to be MOST consistent with the modern systems approach? Training can be effective ONLY when it is
   A. related to the individual abilities of the employees
   B. done on all levels of the organizational hierarchy
   C. evaluated on the basis of experimental and control groups
   D. provided on the job by the immediate supervisor

8. The management of a large agency, before making a decision as to whether or not to computerize its operations, should have a feasibility study made.
Of the following, the one which is LEAST important to include in such a study is
   A. the current abilities of management and staff to use a computer
   B. projected workloads and changes in objectives of functional units in the agency
   C. the contributions expected of each organizational unit towards achievement of agency objectives
   D. the decision-making activity and informational needs of each management function

9. Managing information covers the creation, collection, processing, storage, and transmission of information that appears in a variety of forms. A supervisor responsible for a statistical unit can be considered, in many respects, an information manager.
Of the following, which would be considered the LEAST important aspect of the information manager's job?
   A. Establishing better information standards and forms
   B. Reducing the amount of unnecessary paperwork performed
   C. Producing progressively greater numbers of informational reports
   D. Developing a greater appreciation for information among management members

9.____

10. Because of the need for improvement in information systems throughout industry and government, various techniques for improving these systems have been developed.
Of these, *systems simulation* is a technique for improving systems which
   A. creates new ideas and concepts through the use of a computer
   B. deals with time controlling of interrelated systems which make up an overall project
   C. permits experimentation with various ideas to see what results might be obtained
   D. does not rely on assumptions which condition the value of the results

10.____

11. The one of the following which it is NOT advisable for a supervisor to do when dealing with individual employees is to
   A. recognize a person's outstanding service as well as his mistakes
   B. help an employee satisfy his need to excel
   C. encourage an efficient employee to seek better opportunities even if this action may cause the supervisor to lose a good worker
   D. take public notice of an employee's mistakes so that fewer errors will be made in the future

11.____

12. Suppose that you are in a department where you are given the responsibility for teaching seven new assistants a number of routine procedures that all assistants should know.
Of the following, the BEST method for you to follow in teaching these procedures is to
   A. separate the slower learners from the faster learners and adapt your presentation to their level of ability
   B. instruct all the new employees in a group without attempting to assess differences in learning rates
   C. restrict your approach to giving them detailed written instructions in order to save time
   D. avoid giving the employees written instructions in order to force them to memorize job procedures quickly

12.____

13. Suppose that you are a supervisor to whom several assistants must hand in work for review. You notice that one of the assistants gets very upset whenever you discover an error in his work, although all the assistants make mistakes from time to time.
Of the following, it would be BEST for you to
   A. arrange discreetly for the employee's work to be reviewed by another supervisor
   B. ignore his reaction since giving attention to such behavior increases its intensity
   C. suggest that the employee seek medical help since he has such great difficulty in accepting normal criticism
   D. try to build the employee's self-confidence by emphasizing those parts of his work that are done well

14. Suppose you are a supervisor responsible for supervising a number of assistants in an agency where each assistant receives a manual of policies and procedures when he first reports for work. You have been asked to teach your subordinates a new procedure which requires knowledge of several items of policy and procedure found in the manual.
The one of the following techniques which it would be BEST for you to employ is to
   A. give verbal instructions which include a review of the appropriate standard procedures as well as an explanation of new tasks
   B. give individual instruction restricted to the new procedure to each assistant as the need arises
   C. provide written instructions for new procedural elements and refer employees to their manuals for explanation of standard procedures
   D. ask employees to review appropriate sections of their manual and then explain those aspects of the new procedure which the manual did not cover

15. Supposes that you are a supervisor in charge of a unit in which changes in work procedures are about to be instituted.
The one of the following which you, as the supervisor, should anticipate as being MOST likely to occur during the changeover is
   A. a temporary rise in production because of interest in the new procedures
   B. uniform acceptance of these procedures on the part of your staff
   C. varying interpretations of the new procedures by your staff
   D. general agreement among staff members that the new procedures are advantageous

16. Suppose that a supervisor and one of the assistants under his supervision are known to be friends who play golf together on weekends.
The maintenance of such a friendship on the part of the supervisor is GENERALLY
   A. *acceptable* as long as this assistant continues to perform his duties satisfactorily
   B. *unacceptable* since the supervisor will find it difficult to treat the assistant as a subordinate

C. *acceptable* if the supervisor does not favor this assistant above other employees
D. *unacceptable* because the other assistants will resent the friendship regardless of the supervisor's behavior on the job

17. Suppose that you are a supervisor assigned to review the financial records of an agency which has recently undergone a major reorganization.
    Which of the following would it be BEST for you to do FIRST?
    A. Interview the individual in charge of agency financial operations to determine whether the organizational changes affect the system of financial review
    B. Discuss the nature of the reorganization with your own supervisor to anticipate and plan a new financial review procedure
    C. Carry out the financial review as usual, and adjust your methods to any problems arising from the reorganization
    D. Request a written report from the agency head explaining the nature of the reorganization and recommending changes in the system of financial review

17.____

18. Suppose that a newly assigned supervisor finds that he must delegate some of his duties to subordinates in order to get the work done.
    Which one of the following would NOT be a block to his delegating these duties effectively?
    A. Inability to give proper directions as to what he wants done
    B. Reluctance to take calculated risks
    C. Lack of trust in his subordinates
    D. Retaining ultimate responsibility for the delegated work

18.____

19. A supervisor sometimes performs the staff function of preparing and circulating reports among bureau chiefs.
    Which of the following is LEAST important as an objective in designing and writing such reports?
    A. Providing relevant information on past, present, and future actions
    B. Modifying his language in order to insure goodwill among the bureau chiefs
    C. Helping the readers of the report to make appropriate decisions
    D. Summarizing important information to help readers see trends or outstanding points

19.____

20. Suppose you are a supervisor assigned to prepare a report to be read by all bureau chiefs in your agency.
    The MOST important reason for avoiding highly technical accounting terminology in writing this report is to
    A. ensure the accuracy and relevancy of the text
    B. insure winning the readers' cooperation
    C. make the report more interesting to the readers
    D. make it easier for the readers to understand

20.____

21. Which of the following conditions is MOST likely to cause low morale in an office?
    A. Different standards of performance for individuals in the same title
    B. A requirement that employees perform at full capacity
    C. Standards of performance that vary with titles of employees
    D. Careful attention to the image of the division or department

22. A wise supervisor or representative of management realizes that, in the relationship between supervisor and subordinates, all power is not on the side of management, and that subordinates do sometimes react to restrictive authority in such a manner as to seriously retard management's objectives. A wise supervisor does not stimulate such reactions.
    In the subordinate's attempt to retaliate against an unusually authoritative management style, which of the following actions would generally be LEAST successful for the subordinate? He
    A. joins with other employees in organizations to deal with management
    B. obviously delays in carrying out instructions which are given in an arrogant or incisive manner
    C. performs assignments exactly as instructed even when he recognizes errors in instructions
    D. holds back the flow of feedback information to superiors

23. Which of the following is the MOST likely and costly effect of vague and indefinite instructions given to subordinates by a supervisor?
    A. Misunderstanding and ineffective work on the part of the subordinates
    B. A necessity for the supervisor to report identical instructions with each assignment
    C. A failure of the supervisor to adequately keep the attention of subordinates
    D. Inability of subordinates to assist each other in the absence of the supervisor

24. At the professional level, there is a kind of informal authority which exercises itself even though no delegation of authority has taken place from higher management. It occurs within the context of knowledge required and professional competence in a special area.
    An example of the kind of authority described in this statement is MOST clearly exemplified in the situation where a senior supervisor influences associates and subordinates by virtue of the
    A. salary level fixed for his particular set of duties
    B. amount of college training he possesses
    C. technical position he has gained and holds on the work team
    D. initiative and judgment he has demonstrated to his supervisor

25. An assistant under your supervision attempts to conceal the fact that he has made an error.
    Under this circumstance, it would be BEST for you, as the supervisor, to proceed on the assumption that

A. this evasion indicates something wrong in the fundamental relationship between you and the assistant
B. this evasion is not deliberate, if the error is subsequently corrected by the assistant
C. this evasion should be overlooked if the error is not significant
D. detection and correction of errors will come about as an automatic consequence of internal control procedures

KEY (CORRECT ANSWERS)

1.	C	11.	D
2.	B	12.	B
3.	C	13.	D
4.	D	14.	A
5.	D	15.	C
6.	B	16.	C
7.	B	17.	A
8.	A	18.	D
9.	C	19.	B
10.	C	20.	D

21.	A
22.	B
23.	A
24.	C
25.	A

TEST 2

DIRECTIONS: Each question or incomplete statement is followed by several suggested answers or completions. Select the one that BEST answers the question or completes the statement. *PRINT THE LETTER OF THE CORRECT ANSWER IN THE SPACE AT THE RIGHT.*

1. The unit which you supervise has a number of attorneys, accountants, examiners, statisticians, and clerks who prepare some of the routine papers required to be filed. In order to be certain that nothing goes out of your office that is improper, you have instituted a system that requires that you review and initial all moving papers, memoranda of law and briefs that are prepared. As a result, you put in a great deal of overtime and even must take work home with you frequently.
A situation such as this is
   A. inevitable if you are to keep proper controls over the quality of the office work product
   B. indicative of the fact that the agency must provide an additional position within your office for an assistant supervisor who would do all the reviewing, leaving you free for other pressing administrative work and to handle the most difficult work in your unit
   C. the logical result of an ever-increasing caseload
   D. symptomatic of poor supervision and management

1.____

2. Your unit has been assigned a new employee who has never worked for the city.
To orient him to his job in your unit, of the following, the BEST procedure is first to
   A. assign him to another employee to whatever work that employee gives him so that he can become familiar with your work and at the same time be productive
   B. give him copies of the charter and code provisions affecting your operations plus any in-office memoranda or instructions that are available and have him read them
   C. assign him to work on a relatively simple problem and then, after he has finished it, tell him politely what he did wrong
   D. explain to him the duties of his position and the functions of the office

2.____

3. A bureau chief who supervises other supervisors makes it a practice to assign them more cases than they can possibly handle.
This approach is
   A. *right*, because it results in getting more work done than would otherwise be the case
   B. *right*, because it relieves the bureau chief making the assignments of the responsibility of getting the work done
   C. *wrong*, because it builds resistance on the part of those called upon to handle the caseload
   D. *wrong*, because superiors lose track of cases

3.____

4. Assume you are a supervisor and are expected to exercise *authority* over subordinates.
   Which of the following BEST defines *authority*? The
   A. ability to control the nature of the contribution a subordinate is desirous of making
   B. innate inability to get others to do for you what you want to get done irrespective of their own wishes
   C. legal right conferred by the agency to control the actions of others
   D. power to determine a subordinate's attitude toward his agency and his superiors

5. Paternalistic leadership stresses a paternal or fatherly influence in the relationships between the leader and the group and is manifest in a watchful care for the comfort and welfare of the followers.
   Which one of the following statements regarding paternalistic leadership is MOST accurate?
   A. Employees who work well under paternalistic leadership come to expect such leadership even when the paternal leader has left the organization.
   B. Most disputes arising out of supervisor-subordinate relationships develop because group leaders do not understand the principles of paternalistic leadership.
   C. Paternalistic leadership frequently destroys office relationships because most employees are turned into non-thinking dependent robots.
   D. Paternalistic leadership is rarely, if ever, successful because employees resent paternalistic leadership which they equate with weakness.

6. Employees who have extensive dealings with members of the public should have, as much as possible, *real acceptance* of all people and a willingness to serve everyone impartially and objectively.
   Assuming that this statement is correct, the one of the following which would be the BEST demonstration of *real acceptance* is
   A. condoning antisocial behavior
   B. giving the appearance of agreeing with everyone encountered
   C. refusing to give opinions on anyone's behavior
   D. understanding the feelings expressed through a person's behavior

7. Assume that the agency chief has requested you to help plan a public relations program because of recent complaints from citizens about the unbecoming conduct and language of various groups of city employees who have dealings with the public.
   In carrying out this assignment, the one of the following steps which should be undertaken FIRST is to
   A. study the characteristics of the public clientele dealt with by employees in your agency
   B. arrange to have employees attend several seminars on human relations
   C. develop several procedures for dealing with the public and allow the staff to choose the one which is best
   D. find out whether the employees in your agency may oppose any plan proposed by you

8. The one of the following statements which BEST expresses the relationship between the morale of government employees and the public relations aspects of their work is:
   A. There is little relationship between employee morale and public relations, chiefly because public opinion is shaped primarily by response to departmental policy formulation.
   B. Employee morale is closely related to public relations, chiefly because the employee's morale will largely determine the manner in which he deals with the public.
   C. There is little relationship between employee morale and public relations, chiefly because public relations is primarily a function of the agency's public relations department.
   D. Employee morale is closely related to public relations, chiefly because employee morale indicates the attitude of the agency's top officials toward the public.

9. As a supervisor, you are required to deal extensively with the public. The agency chief has indicated that he is considering holding a special in-service training course for employees in communications skills
   Holding this training course would be
   A. *advisable*, chiefly because government employees should receive formal training in public relations skills
   B. *inadvisable*, chiefly because the public regards such training as a *waste of the taxpayers money*
   C. *advisable*, chiefly because such training will enable the employee to aid in drafting departmental press releases
   D. *inadvisable*, chiefly because of the great difficulty involved in developing skills through formal instruction

10. Assume that you have extensive contact with the public. In dealing with the public, sensitivity to an individual's attitudes is important because these attitudes can be used to predict behavior.
    However, the MAIN reason that attitudes CANNOT successfully predict all behavior is that
    A. attitudes are highly resistant to change
    B. an individual acquires attitudes as a function of growing up in a particular cultural environment
    C. attitudes are only one of many factors which determine a person's behavior
    D. an individual's behavior is not always observable

11. Rotation of employees from assignment to assignment is sometimes advocated by management experts.
    Of the following, the MOST probable advantage to the organization of this practice is that it leads to
    A. higher specialization of duties so that excessive identification with the overall organization is reduced
    B. increased loyalty of employees to their immediate supervisors

C. greater training and development of employees
D. intensified desire of employees to obtain additional, outside formal education

12. Usually, a supervisor should attempt to standardize the work for which he is responsible.
    The one of the following which is a BASIC reason for doing this is to
    A. eliminate the need to establish priorities
    B. permit the granting of exceptions to rules and special circumstances
    C. facilitate the taking of action based on applicable standards
    D. learn the identity of outstanding employees

12.____

13. The differences between line and staff authority are often quite ambiguous. Of the following, the ESSENTIAL difference is that
    A. *line authority* is exercised by first-level supervisors; *staff authority* is exercised by higher-level supervisors and managerial staff
    B. *staff authority* is the right to issue directives; *line authority* is entirely consultative
    C. *line authority* is the power to make decisions regarding intra-agency matters; *staff authority* involves decisions regarding inter-agency matters
    D. *staff authority* is largely advisory; *line authority* is the right to command

13.____

14. Modern management theory stresses work-centered motivation as one way of increasing the productivity of employees.
    The one of the following which is PARTICULARLY characteristic of such motivation is that it
    A. emphasizes the crucial role of routinization of procedures
    B. stresses the satisfaction to be found in performing work
    C. features the value of wages and fringe benefits
    D. uses a firm but fair method of discipline

14.____

15. The agency's informal communications network is called the *grapevine*.
    If employees are learning about important organizational developments primarily through the grapevine, this is MOST likely an indication that
    A. official channels of communication are not functioning so efficiently as they should
    B. supervisory personnel are making effective use of the grapevine to communicate with subordinates
    C. employees already have a clear understanding of the agency's policies and procedures
    D. upward formal channels of communication within the agency are informing management of employee grievances

15.____

16. Of the following, a flow chart is BEST described as a chart which shows
    A. the places through which work moves in the course of the job process
    B. which employees perform specific functions leading to the completion of a job

16.____

C. the schedules for production and how they eliminate waiting time between jobs
D. how work units are affected by the actions of related work units

17. Evaluation of the results of training is necessary in order to assess its value. 17.____
Of the following, the BEST technique for the supervisor to use in determining whether the training under consideration actually resulted in the desired modification of the behavior of the employee concerned is through
  A. inference B. job analysis C. observation D. simulation

18. The usual distinction between line and staff authority is that staff authority is 18.____
mainly advisory, whereas line authority is the right to command. However, a third category has been suggested-prescriptive-to distinguish those personnel whose functions may be formally defined as staff but in practice exercise considerable authority regarding decisions relating to their specialties.
The one of the following which indicates the MAJOR purpose of creating this third category is to
  A. develop the ability of each employee to perform a greater number of tasks
  B. reduce line-staff conflict
  C. prevent over-specialization of functions
  D. encourage decision-making by line personnel

19. It is sometimes considered desirable to train employees to a standard of 19.____
proficiency higher than that deemed necessary for actual job performance.
The MOST likely reason for such overtraining would be to
  A. eliminate the need for standards
  B. increase the value of refresher training
  C. compensate for previous lack of training
  D. reduce forgetting or loss of skill

20. Assume that you have been directed to immediately institute various new 20.____
procedures in the handling of records.
Of the following, the BEST method for you to use to insure that your subordinates know exactly what to do is to
  A. circulate a memorandum explaining the new procedure have your subordinates initial it
  B. explain the new procedures to one or two subordinates and ask them to tell the others
  C. have a meeting with your subordinates to give them copies of the procedures and discuss it with them
  D. post the new procedures where they can be referred to by all those concerned

21. A supervisor decided to hold a problem-solving conference with his entire staff and distributed an announcement and agenda one week before the meeting.
Of the following, the BEST reason for providing each participant with an agenda is that
    A. participants will feel that something will be accomplished
    B. participants may prepare for the conference
    C. controversy will be reduced
    D. the top man should state the expected conclusions

22. In attempting to motivate employees, rewards are considered preferable to punishment PRIMARILY because
    A. punishment seldom has any effect on human behavior
    B. punishment usually results in decreased production
    C. supervisors find it difficult to punish
    D. rewards are more likely to result in willing cooperation

23. In an attempt to combat the low morale in his organization, a high-level supervisor publicized an *open-door* policy to allow employees who wished to do so to come to him with their complaints.
Which of the following is LEAST likely to account for the fact that no employee came in with a complaint?
    A. Employees are generally reluctant to go over the heads of their immediate supervisors.
    B. The employees did not feel that management would help them.
    C. The low morale was not due to complaints association with the job
    D. The employees felt that they had more to lose than to gain.

24. It is MOST desirable to use written instructions rather than oral instructions for a particular job when
    A. a mistake on the job will not be serious
    B. the job can be completed in a short time
    C. there is no need to explain the job minutely
    D. the job involves many details

25. You have been asked to prepare for public distribution a statement dealing with a controversial matter.
Of the following approaches, the one which would usually be MOST effective is to present your department's point of view
    A. as tersely as possible with no reference to any other matters
    B. developed from ideas and facts well known to most readers
    C. and show all the statistical data and techniques which were used in arriving at it
    D. in such a way that the controversial parts are omitted

KEY (CORRECT ANSWERS)

1. D
2. D
3. C
4. C
5. A

6. D
7. A
8. B
9. A
10. C

11. C
12. C
13. D
14. B
15. A

16. A
17. C
18. B
19. D
20. C

21. B
22. D
23. C
24. D
25. B

TEST 3

DIRECTIONS: Each question or incomplete statement is followed by several suggested answers or completions. Select the one that BEST answers the question or completes the statement. *PRINT THE LETTER OF THE CORRECT ANSWER IN THE SPACE AT THE RIGHT.*

1. An administrator who supervises other supervisors makes it a practice to set deadline dates for completion of assignments.
   A NATURAL consequence of setting deadline dates is that
   A. supervisors will usually wait until the deadline date before they give projects their wholehearted attention
   B. projects are completed sooner than if no deadline dates are set
   C. such dates are ignored even though they are conspicuously posted
   D. the frequency of errors sharply increases resulting in an inability to meet deadlines

   1._____

2. Assume that you are chairing a meeting of the members of your staff. You throw out a question to the group. No one answers your question immediately, so that you find yourself faced with silence.
   In the circumstances, it would probably be BEST for you to
   A. ask the member of the group who appears to be least attentive to repeat the question
   B. change the topic quickly
   C. repeat the question carefully, pronouncing each word, and if there is still no response, repeat the question an additional time
   D. wait for an answer since someone will usually say something to break the tension

   2._____

3. Assume that you are holding a meeting with the members of your staff. John, a member of the unit, keeps sidetracking the subject of the discussion by bringing up extraneous matters. You deal with the situation by saying to him after he has raised an immaterial point, *"That's an interesting point John, but can you show me how it ties in with what we're talking about?"*
   Your approach in this situation would GENERALLY be considered
   A. *bad*; you have prevented the group from discussing not only extraneous matters but pertinent material as well
   B. *bad*; you have seriously humiliated John in front of the entire group
   C. *good*; you have pointed out how the discussion is straying from the main topic
   D. *good*; you have prevented John from presenting extraneous matters at future meetings

   3._____

4. Assume that a senior supervisor is asked to supervise a group of staff personnel. The work of one of these staff men meets minimum standards of acceptability. However, this staff man constantly looks for something at which to take offense. In any conversation with either a fellow staff man or with a superior, he views the slightest criticism as a grave insult.

   4._____

73

In this case, the senior supervisor should
- A. advise the staff man that the next time he refuses to accept criticism, he will be severely reprimanded
- B. ask member of the group for advice on how to deal with this staff man
- C. make it a practice to speak calmly, slowly, and deliberately to this staff man and question him frequently to make sure that there is no breakdown in communications
- D. recognize that professional help may be required and that this problem may not be conducive to a solution by a supervisor

5. Assume that you discover that one of the staff in preparing certain papers has made a serious mistake which has become obvious.
In dealing with this situation, it would be BEST for you to begin by
- A. asking the employee how the mistake happened
- B. asking the employee to read through the papers to see whether he can correct the mistake
- C. pointing out to the employee that, while an occasional error is permissible, frequent errors can prove a source of embarrassment to all concerned
- D. pointing to the mistake and asking the employee whether he realizes the consequences of the mistake

6. You desire to develop teamwork among the members of your staff. You are assigned a case which will require that two of the staff work together if the papers are to be prepared in time. You decided to assign two employees, whom you know to be close friends, to work on these papers.
Your action in this regard would GENERALLY be considered
- A. *bad*; friends working together tend to do as little as they can get away with
- B. *bad*; people who are friends socially often find that the bonds of friendship disintegrate in work situations
- C. *good*; friends who are permitted to work together show their appreciation by utilizing every opportunity to reinforce the group leader's position of authority
- D. *good*; the evidence suggests that more work can be done in this way

7. You notice that all of the employees, without exception, take lunch hours which in your view are excessively long. You call each of them to your desk and point out that unless this practice is brought to a stop, appropriate action will be taken.
The way in which you handled this problem would GENERALLY be considered
- A. *proper*, primarily because a civil servant, no matter what his professional status, owes the public a full day's work for a full day's pay
- B. *proper*, primarily because employees need to have a clear picture of the rewards and penalties that go with public employment
- C. *improper*, primarily because group problems require group discussion which need not be formal in character
- D. *improper*, primarily because professional personnel resent having such matters as lunch hours brought to their attention

8. In communicating with superiors or subordinates, it is well to bear in mind a phenomenon known as the *halo effect*. An example of this *halo effect* occurs when we
   A. employ informal language in a formal setting as a means of attracting attention
   B. ignore the advice of someone we distrust without evaluating the advice
   C. ask people to speak up who have a tendency to speak softly or occasionally indistinctly
   D. react to a piece of good work by inquiring into the motivations of those who did the work

8.____

9. Which of the following dangers is MOST likely to arise when a work group becomes too tightly knit? The
   A. group may appoint an informal leader who gradually sets policies and standards for the group to the detriment of the agency
   B. group may be reluctant to accept new employees as members
   C. quantity and quality of work produced may tend to diminish sharply despite the group's best efforts
   D. group may focus too strongly on employee benefits at inappropriate times

9.____

10. The overall managerial problem has become more complex because each group of management specialists will tend to view the interests of the enterprise in terms which are compatible with the survival or the increase of its special function. That is, each group will have a trained capacity for its own function and a *trained incapacity* to see its relation to the whole.
    The *trained incapacity* to which the foregoing passage refers PROBABLY results from
    A. an imbalance in the number of specialists as compared with the number of generalists
    B. development by each specialized group of a certain dominant value or goal that shapes its entire way of doing things
    C. low morale accompanied by lackadaisical behavior by large segments of the managerial staff
    D. supervisory failure to inculcate pride in workmanship

10.____

11. Of the following, the MOST important responsibility of a supervisor in charge of a section is to
    A establish close personal relationships with each of his subordinates in the section
    B. insure that each subordinate in the section knows the full range of his duties and responsibilities
    C. maintain friendly relations with his immediate supervisor
    D. protect his subordinates from criticism from any source

11.____

12. The BEST way to get a good work output from employees is to
    A. hold over them the threat of disciplinary action or removal
    B. maintain a steady, unrelenting pressure on them
    C. show them that you can do anything they can do faster and better
    D win their respect and liking so they want to work for you

12.____

13. Supervisors should GENERALLY
    A. lean more toward management than toward their subordinates
    B. lean neither toward subordinates nor management
    C. lean more toward their subordinates than toward their management
    D. maintain a proper balance between management and subordinates

14. For a supervisor in charge of a section to ask occasionally the opinion of a subordinate concerning a problem is
    A. *desirable*; but it would be even better if the subordinate were consulted routinely on every problem
    B. *desirable*; subordinates may make good suggestions and will be pleased by being consulted
    C. *undesirable*; subordinates may be resentful if their advice is not followed
    D. *undesirable*; the supervisor should not attempt to shift his responsibilities to subordinates

15. The PRIMARY responsibility of a supervisor is to
    A. gain the confidence and make friends of all his subordinates
    B. get the work done properly
    C. satisfy his superior and gain his respect
    D. train the men in new methods for doing the work

16. In starting a work simplification study, the one of the following steps that should be taken FIRST is to
    A. break the work down into its elements
    B. draw up a chart of operations
    C. enlist the interest and cooperation of the personnel
    D. suggest alternative procedures

17. Of the following, the MOST important value of a manual of procedures is that it usually
    A. eliminates the need for on-the-job training
    B. decreases the span of control which can be exercised by individual supervisory personnel
    C. outlines methods of operation for ready reference
    D. provides concrete examples of work previously performed by employees

18. Reprimanding a subordinate when he has done something wrong should be done PRIMARILY in order to
    A. deter others from similar acts
    B. improve the subordinate in future performance
    C. maintain discipline
    D. uphold departmental rules

19. Most of the training of new employees in a public agency is USUALLY accomplished by
    A. formal classes   B. general orientation
    C. internship   D. on-the-job activities

5 (#3)

20. You find that delivery of a certain item cannot possibly be made to a using agency by the date the using agency requested.
    Of the following, the MOST advisable course of action for you to take FIRST is to
    A. cancel the order and inform the using agency
    B. discuss the problem with the using agency
    C. notify the using agency to obtain the item through direct purchase
    D. schedule the delivery for the earliest possible date

20.____

21. Assume that one of your subordinates has gotten into the habit of regularly and routinely referring every small problem which arises in his work to you.
    In order to help him overcome this habit, it is generally MOST advisable for you to
    A. advise him that you do not have time to discuss each problem with him and that he should do whatever he wants
    B. ask your subordinate for his solution and approve any satisfactory approach that he suggests
    C. refuse to discuss such routine problems with him
    D. tell him that he should consider looking for another position if he does not feel competent to solve such routine problems

21.____

22. The BEST of the following reasons for developing understudies to supervisory staff is that this practice
    A. assures that capable staff will not leave their jobs since they are certain to be promoted
    B. helps to assure continued efficiency when persons in important positions leave their jobs
    C. improves morale by demonstrating to employees the opportunities for advancement
    D. provides an opportunity for giving on-the-job training

22.____

23. When a supervisor delegates some of his work to a subordinate, the
    A. supervisor retains final responsibility for the work
    B. supervisor should not check on the work until it has been completed
    C. subordinate assumes full responsibility for the successful completion of the work
    D. subordinate is likely to lose interest and get less satisfaction from the work

23.____

24. Sometimes it is necessary to give out written orders or to post written or typed information on a bulletin board rather than to merely give spoken orders. The supervisor must decide how he will do it.
    In which of the following situations would it be BETTER for him to give written rather than spoken orders?
    A. He is going to reassign a man from one unit to another under his supervision.
    B. His staff must be informed of a permanent change in a complicated operating procedure.

24.____

C. A man must be transferred from a clerical unit to an operating unit.
D. He must order a group of staff men to do a difficult and tedious inventory job to which most of them are likely to object.

25. Of the following symbolic patterns, which one is NOT representative of a normal direction in which formal organizational communications flow? 25.____

A. I B. II C. III D. IV

KEY (CORRECT ANSWERS)

1. B
2. D
3. C
4. D
5. A

6. D
7. C
8. B
9. B
10. B

11. B
12. D
13. D
14. B
15. B

16. C
17. C
18. B
19. D
20. B

21. B
22. B
23. A
24. B
25. B

EXAMINATION SECTION
TEST 1

DIRECTIONS: Each question or incomplete statement is followed by several suggested answers or completions. Select the one that BEST answers the question or completes the statement. *PRINT THE LETTER OF THE CORRECT ANSWER IN THE SPACE AT THE RIGHT.*

1. Which one of the following generalizations is MOST likely to be INACCURATE and lead to judgmental errors in communication?
    A. A supervisor must be able to read with understanding.
    B. Misunderstanding may lead to dislike.
    C. Anyone can listen to another person and understand what he means.
    D. It is usually desirable to let a speaker talk until he is finished.

2. Assume that, as a supervisor, you have been directed to inform your subordinates about the implementation of a new procedure which will affect their work.
   While communicating this information, you should do all of the following EXCEPT
    A. obtain the approval of your subordinates regarding the new procedure
    B. explain the reason for implementing the new procedure
    C. hold a staff meeting at a time convenient to most of your subordinates
    D. encourage a productive discussion of the new procedure

3. Assume that you are in charge of a section that handles requests for information on matters received from the public. One day, you observe that a clerk under your supervision is using a method to log-in requests for information that is different from the one specified by you in the past. Upon questioning the clerk, you discover that instructions changing the old procedure were delivered orally by your supervisor on a day on which you were absent from the office.
   Of the following, the MOST appropriate action for you to take is to
    A. tell the clerk to revert to the old procedure at once
    B. ask your supervisor for information about the change
    C. call your staff together and tell them that no existing procedure is to be changed unless you direct that it be done
    D. write a memo to your supervisor suggesting that all future changes in procedure are to be in writing and that they be directed to you

4. At the first meeting with your staff after appointment as a supervisor, you find considerable indifference and some hostility among the participants.
   Of the following, the MOST appropriate way to handle this situation is to
    A. disregard the attitudes displayed and continue to make your presentation until you have completed it
    B. discontinue your presentation but continue the meeting and attempt to find out the reasons for their attitudes

C. warm up your audience with some good-natured statements and anecdotes and then proceed with your presentation
D. discontinue the meeting and set up personal interviews with the staff members to try to find out the reason for their attitude

5. In order to start the training of a new employee, it has been a standard practice to have him read a manual of instructions or procedures.
   This method is currently being replaced by the _____ method.
   A. audio-visual
   B. conference
   C. lecture
   D. programmed instruction

5.____

6. Of the following subjects, the one that can usually be successfully taught by a first-line supervisor who is training his subordinates is:
   A. theory and philosophy of management
   B. human relations
   C. responsibilities of a supervisor
   D. job skills

6.____

7. Assume that as supervisor you are training a clerk who is experiencing difficulty learning a new task.
   Which of the following would be the LEAST effective approach to take when trying to solve this problem? To
   A. ask questions which will reveal the clerk's understanding of the task
   B. take a different approach in explaining the task
   C. give the clerk an opportunity to ask questions about the task
   D. make sure the clerk knows you are watching his work closely

7.____

8. One school of management and supervision involves participation by employees in the setting of group goals and in the sharing of responsibility for the operation of the unit.
   If this philosophy were applied to a unit consisting of professional and clerical personnel, one should expect
   A. the professional and clerical personnel to participate with equal effectiveness in operating areas and policy areas
   B. the professional personnel to participate with greater effectiveness than the clerical personnel in policy areas
   C. the clerical personnel to participate with greater effectiveness than the professional personnel in operating areas
   D. greater participation by clerical personnel but with less responsibility for their actions

8.____

9. With regard to productivity, high morale among employees generally indicates a
   A. history of high productivity
   B. nearly absolute positive correlation with high productivity
   C. predisposition to be productive under facilitating leadership and circumstances
   D. complacency which has little effect on productivity

9.____

10. Assume that you are going to organize the professionals and clerks under your supervision into work groups or team of two or three employees.
    Of the following, the step which is LEAST likely to foster the successful development of each group is to
    A. allow friends to work together in the group
    B. provide special help and attention to employees with no friends in their group
    C. frequently switch employees from group to group
    D. rotate jobs within the group in order to strengthen group identification

11. Following are four statements which might be made by an employee to his supervisor during a performance evaluation interview.
    Which of the statements BEST provides a basis for developing a plan to improve the employee's performance?
    A. *I understand that you are dissatisfied with my work and I will try harder in the future.*
    B. *I feel that I've been making too many careless clerical errors recently.*
    C. *I am aware that I will be subject to disciplinary action if my work does not improve within one month.*
    D. *I understand that this interview is simply a requirement of your job and not a personal attack on me.*

12. Three months ago, Mr. Smith and his supervisor, Mrs. Jones, developed a plan which was intended to correct Mr. Smith's inadequate job performance. Now, during a follow-up interview, Mr. Smith, who thought his performance had satisfactorily improved, has been informed that Mrs. Jones is still dissatisfied with his work.
    Of the following, it is MOST likely that the disagreement occurred because, when formulating the plan, they did NOT
    A. set realistic goals for Mr. Smith's performance
    B. set a reasonable time limit for Mr. Smith to effect his improvement in performance
    C. provide for adequate training to improve Mr. Smith's skills
    D. establish performance standards for measuring Mr. Smith's progress

13. When a supervisor delegates authority to subordinates, there are usually many problems to overcome, such as inadequately trained subordinates and poor planning.
    All of the following are means of increasing the effectiveness of delegation EXCEPT:
    A. Defining assignments in the light of results expected
    B. Maintaining open lines of communication
    C. Establishing tight controls so that subordinates will stay within the bounds of the area of delegation
    D. Providing rewards for successful assumption of authority by a subordinate

4 (#1)

14. Assume that one of your subordinates has arrived late for work several times during the current month. The last time he was late you had warned him that another unexcused lateness would result informal disciplinary action.
If the employee arrives late for work again during this month, the FIRST action you should take is to
    A. give the employee a chance to explain this lateness
    B. give the employee a written copy of your warning
    C. tell the employee that you are recommending formal disciplinary action
    D. tell the employee that you will give him only one more chance before recommending formal disciplinary action

14.____

15. In trying to decide how many subordinates a manager can control directly, one of the determinants is how much the manager can reduce the frequency and time consumed in contacts with his subordinates.
Of the following, the factor which LEAST influences the number and direction of these contacts is:
    A. How well the manager delegates authority
    B. The rate at which the organization is changing
    C. The control techniques used by the manager
    D. Whether the activity is line or staff

15.____

16. Systematic rotation of employees through lateral transfer within a government organization to provide for managerial development is
    A. *good*, because systematic rotation develops specialists who learn to do many jobs well
    B. *bad*, because the outsider upsets the status quo of the existing organization
    C. *good*, because rotation provides challenge and organizational flexibility
    D. *bad*, because it is upsetting to employees to be transferred within a service

16.____

17. Assume that you are required to provide an evaluation of the performance of your subordinates.
Of the following factors, it is MOST important that the performance evaluation include a rating of each employee's
    A. initiative   B. productivity   C. intelligence   D. personality

17.____

18. When preparing performance evaluations of your subordinates, one way to help assure that you are rating each employee fairly is to
    A. prepare a list of all employees and all the rating factors and rate all employees on one rating factor before going on to the next factor
    B. prepare a list of all your employees and all the rating factors and rate each employee on all factors before going on to the next employee
    C. discuss all the ratings you anticipate giving with another supervisor in order to obtain an unbiased opinion
    D. discuss each employee with his co-workers in order to obtain peer judgment of worth before doing any rating

18.____

5 (#1)

19. A managerial plan which would include the GREATEST control is a plan which is 19._____
    A. spontaneous and geared to each new job that is received
    B. detailed and covering an extended time period
    C. long-range and generalized, allowing for various interpretations
    D. specific and prepared daily

20. Assume that you are preparing a report which includes statistical data covering 20._____
    increases in budget allocations of four agencies for the past ten years.
    For you to represent the statistical data pictorially or graphically within the
    report is a
    A. *poor* idea, because you should be able to make statistical data
       understandable through the use of words
    B. *good* idea, because it is easier for the reader to understand pictorial
       representation rather than quantities of words conveying statistical data
    C. *poor* idea, because using pictorial representation in a report may make
       the report too expensive to print
    D. *good* idea, because a pictorial representation makes the report appear
       more attractive than the use of many words to convey the statistical data

---

KEY (CORRECT ANSWERS)

1.	C	11.	A
2.	A	12.	B
3.	B	13.	C
4.	D	14.	A
5.	D	15.	D
6.	D	16.	C
7.	D	17.	B
8.	B	18.	A
9.	C	19.	B
10.	C	20.	B

TEST 2

DIRECTIONS: Each question or incomplete statement is followed by several suggested answers or completions. Select the one that BEST answers the question or completes the statement. *PRINT THE LETTER OF THE CORRECT ANSWER IN THE SPACE AT THE RIGHT.*

1. Research studies have shown that supervisors of groups with high production records USUALLY
    A. give detailed instructions, constantly check on progress, and insist on approval of all decisions before implementation
    B. do considerable paperwork and other work similar to that performed by subordinates
    C. think of themselves as team members on the same level as others in the work group
    D. perform tasks traditionally associated with managerial functions

1.____

2. Mr. Smith, a bureau chief, is summoned by his agency's head in a conference to discuss Mr. Jones, an accountant who works in one of the divisions of his bureau. Mr. Jones has committed an error of such magnitude as to arouse the agency head's concern.
After agreeing with the other conferees that a severe reprimand would be the appropriate punishment, Mr. Smith SHOULD
    A. arrange for Mr. Jones to explain the reasons for his error to the agency head
    B. send a memorandum to Mr. Jones, being careful that the language emphasizes the nature of the error rather than Mr. Jones' personal faults
    C. inform Mr. Jones' immediate supervisor of the conclusion reached at the conference, and let the supervisor take the necessary action
    D. suggest to the agency head that no additional action be taken against Mr. Jones because no further damage will be caused by the error

2.____

3. Assume that Ms. Thomson, a unit chief, has determined that the findings of an internal audit have been seriously distorted as a result of careless errors. The audit had been performed by a group of auditors in her unit and the errors were overlooked by the associate accountant in charge of the audit. Ms. Thomson has decided to delay discussing the matter with the associate accountant and the staff who performed the audit until she verifies certain details, which may require prolonged investigation.
Mrs. Thomson's method of handling this situation is
    A. *appropriate*; employees should not be accused of wrongdoing until all the facts have been determined
    B. *inappropriate*; the employees involved may assume that the errors were considered unimportant
    C. *appropriate*; employees are more likely to change their behavior as a result of disciplinary action taken after a *cooling off* period
    D. *inappropriate*; the employees involved may have forgotten the details and become emotionally upset when confronted with the facts

3.____

4. After studying the financial situation in his agency, an administrative accountant decides to recommend centralization of certain accounting functions which are being performed in three different bureaus of the organization
The one of the following which is MOST likely to be a DISADVANTAE if this recommendation is implemented is that
   A. there may be less coordination of the accounting procedure because central direction is not so close to the day-to-day problems as the personnel handling them in each specialized accounting unit
   B. the higher management levels would not be able to make emergency decisions in as timely a manner as the more involved, lower-level administrators who are closer to the problem
   C. it is more difficult to focus the attention of the top management in order to resolve accounting problems because of the many other activities top management is involved in at the same time
   D. the accuracy of upward and inter-unit communication may be reduced because centralization may require insertion of more levels of administration in the chain of command

5. Of the following assumptions about the role of conflict in an organization, the one which is the MOST accurate statement of the approach of modern management theorists is that conflict
   A. can usually be avoided or controlled
   B. serves as a vital element in organizational change
   C. works against attainment of organizational goals
   D. provides a constructive outlet for problem employees

6. Which of the following is generally regarded as the BEST approach for a supervisor to follow in handling grievances brought by subordinates?
   A. Avoid becoming involved personally
   B. Involve the union representative in the first stage of discussion
   C. Settle the grievance as soon as possible
   D. Arrange for arbitration by a third party

7. Assume that supervisors of similar-sized accounting units in city, state, and federal offices were interviewed and observed at their work. It was found that the ways they acted in and viewed their roles tended to be very similar, regardless of who employed them.
Which of the following is the BEST explanation of this similarity
   A. A supervisor will ordinarily behave in conformance to his own self-image.
   B. Each role in an organization, including the supervisory role, calls for a distinct type of personality.
   C. The supervisor role reflects an exceptionally complex pattern of human response.
   D. The general nature of the duties and responsibilities of the supervisory position determines the role.

8. Which of the following is NOT consistent with the findings of recent research about the characteristics of successful top managers?
   A. They are *inner-directed* and not overly concerned with pleasing others.
   B. They are challenged by situations filled with high risk and ambiguity.
   C. They tend to stay on the same job for long periods of time.
   D. They consider it more important to handle critical assignments successfully than to do routine work well.

9. As a supervisor, you have to give subordinates operational guidelines.
   Of the following, the BEST reason for providing them with information about the overall objectives within which their operations fit is that the subordinates will
   A. be more likely to carry out the operation according to your expectations
   B. know that there is a legitimate reason for carrying out the operation in the way you have prescribed
   C. be more likely to handle unanticipated problems that may arise without having to take up your time
   D. more likely to transmit the operating instructions correctly to their subordinates

10. A supervisor holds frequent meetings with his staff.
    Of the following, the BEST approach he can take in order to elicit productive discussions at these meetings is for him to
    A. ask questions of those who attend
    B. include several levels of supervisors at the meetings
    C. hold the meetings at a specified time each week
    D. begin each meeting with a statement that discussion is welcomed

11. Of the following, the MOST important action that a supervisor can take to increase the productivity of a subordinate is to
    A. increase his uninterrupted work time
    B. increase the number of reproducing machines available in the office
    C. provide clerical assistance whenever he requests it
    D. reduce the number of his assigned tasks

12. Assume that, as a supervisor, you find out that you often must countermand or modify your original staff memos.
    If this practice continues, which one of the following situations is MOST likely to occur? The
    A. staff will not bother to read your memos
    B. office files will become cluttered
    C. staff will delay acting on your memos
    D. memos will be treated routinely

13. In making management decisions, the committee approach is often used by managers.
    Of the following, the BEST reason for using this approach is to
    A. prevent any one individual from assuming too much authority
    B. allow the manager to bring a wider range of experience and judgment to bear on the problem

4 (#2)

  C. allow the participation of all staff members, which will make them feel more committed to the decisions reached
  D. permit the rapid transmission of information about decisions reached to the staff members concerned

14. In establishing standards for the measurement of the performance of a management project team, it is MOST important for the project manager to
  A. identify and define the objectives of the project
  B. determine the number of people who will be assigned to the project team
  C. evaluate the skills of the staff who will be assigned to the project team
  D. estimate fairly accurately the length of time required to complete each phase of the project

14.____

15. It is virtually impossible to tell an employee either that he is not good as another employee or that he does not measure up to a desirable level of performance, without having him feel threatened, rejected, and discouraged.
In accordance with the foregoing observation, a supervisor who is concerned about the performance of the less efficient members of his staff should realize that
  A. he might obtain better results by not discussing the quality and quantity of their work with them, but by relying instead on the written evaluation of their performance to motivate their improvement
  B. since he is required to discuss their performance with them, he should do so in words of encouragement and in so friendly a manner as to not destroy their morale
  C. he might discuss their work in a general way, without mentioning any of the specifics about the quality of their performance, with the expectation that they would understand the full implications of his talk
  D. he should make it a point, while telling them of their poor performance, to mention that their work is as good as that of some of the other employees in the unit

15.____

16. Some advocates of management-by-objectives procedures in public agencies have been urging that this method of operations be expanded to encompass all agencies of the government, for one or more of the following reasons, not all of which may be correct:
  I. The MBO method is likely to succeed because it embraces the practice of setting near-term goals for the subordinate manager, reviewing accomplishments at an appropriate time, and repeating this process indefinitely
  II. Provision for authority to perform the tasks assigned as goals in the MBO method is normally not needed because targets are set in quantitative or qualitative terms and specific times for accomplishment are arranged in short-term, repetitive intervals
  III. Many other appraisal-of-performance programs failed because both supervisors and subordinates resisted them, while the MBO approach is not instituted until there is an organizational commitment to it
  IV. Personal accountability is clearly established through the MBO approach because verifiable results are set up in the process of formulating the targets

16.____

Which of the choices below includes ALL of the foregoing statements that are CORRECT?
A. I, III B. II, IV C. I, II, III, IV D. I, III, IV

17. In preparing an organizational structure, the PRINCIPAL guideline for locating staff units is to place them
    A. all under a common supervisor
    B. as close as possible to the activities they serve
    C. as close to the chief executive as possible without over-extending his span of control
    D. at the lowest operational level

17.____

18. The relative importance of any unit in a department can be LEAST reliably judged by the
    A. amount of office space allocated to the unit
    B. number of employees in the unit
    C. rank of the individual who heads the unit
    D. rank of the individual to whom the unit head reports directly

18.____

19. Those who favor Planning-Programming-Budgeting Systems (PPBS) as a new method of governmental financial administration emphasize that PPBS
    A. applies statistical measurements which correlate highly with criteria
    B. makes possible economic systems analysis, including an explicit examination of alternatives
    C. makes available scarce government resources which can be coordinated on a government-wide basis and shared between local units of government
    D. shifts the emphasis in budgeting methods to an automated system of data processing

19.____

20. The term applied to computer processing which processes data concurrently with a given activity and provides results soon enough to influence the selection of a course of action is _____ processing.
    A. realtime   B. batch
    C. random access   D. integrated data

20.____

KEY (CORRECT ANSWERS)

1.	D	11.	A
2.	C	12.	C
3.	B	13.	B
4.	D	14.	A
5.	B	15.	B
6.	C	16.	D
7.	D	17.	B
8.	C	18.	B
9.	C	19.	B
10.	A	20.	A

READING COMPREHENSION
UNDERSTANDING AND INTERPRETING WRITTEN MATERIAL
EXAMINATION SECTION
TEST 1

DIRECTIONS: Each question or incomplete statement is followed by several suggested answers or completions. Select the one that BEST answers the question or completes the statement. *PRINT THE LETTER OF THE CORRECT ANSWER IN THE SPACE AT THE RIGHT.*

Questions 1-5.

DIRECTIONS: Questions 1 through 5 are to be answered SOLELY on the basis of the following passage.

    The most effective control mechanism to prevent gross incompetence on the part of public employees is a good personnel program. The personnel officer in the line departments and the central personnel agency should exert positive leadership to raise levels of performance. Although the key factor is the quality of the personnel recruited, staff members other than personnel officers can make important contributions to efficiency. Administrative analysts, now employed in many agencies, make detailed studies of organization and procedures, with the purpose of eliminating delays, waste, and other inefficiencies. Efficiency is, however, more than a question of good organization and procedures; it is also the product of the attitudes and value of the public employees. Personal motivation can provide the will to be efficient. The best management studies will not result in substantial improvement of the performance of those employees who feel no great urge to wok up to their abilities.

1. The above passage indicates that the KEY factor in preventing gross incompetence of public employees is the
    A. hiring of administrative analysts to assist personnel people
    B. utilization of effective management studies
    C. overlapping of responsibility
    D. quality of the employees hired

1.____

2. According to the above passage, the central personnel agency staff SHOULD
    A. work more closely with administrative analysts in the line departments than with personnel officers
    B. make a serious effort to avoid jurisdictional conflicts with personnel officers in line departments
    C. contribute to improving the quality of work of public employees
    D. engage in a comprehensive program to change the public's negative image of public employees

2.____

3. The above passage indicates that efficiency in an organization can BEST be 3.____
   brought about by
   A. eliminating ineffective control mechanisms
   B. instituting sound organizational procedures
   C. promoting competent personnel
   D. recruiting people with desire to do good work

4. According to the above passage, the purpose of administrative analysts 4.____
   in a public agency is to
   A. prevent injustice to the public employee
   B. promote the efficiency of the agency
   C. protect the interests of the public
   D. ensure the observance of procedural due process

5. The above passage implies that a considerable rise in the quality of work of 5.____
   public employees can be brought about by
   A. encouraging positive employee attitudes toward work
   B. controlling personnel officers who exceed their powers
   C. creating warm personal associations among public employees in an
      agency
   D. closing loopholes in personnel organization and procedures

Questions 6-8.

DIRECTIONS: Questions 6 through 8 are to be answered SOLELY on the basis of the following passage.

EMPLOYEE NEEDS

The greatest waste in industry and in government may be that of human resources. This waste usually derives not from employees' unwillingness or inability, but from management's ineptness to meet the maintenance and motivational needs of employees. Maintenance needs refer to such needs as providing employees with safe places to work, written work rules, job security, adequate salary, employer-sponsored social activities, and with knowledge of their role in the overall framework of the organization. However, of greatest significance to employees are the motivational needs of job growth, achievement, responsibility, and recognition.

Although employee dissatisfaction may stem from either poor maintenance or poor motivation factors, the outward manifestation of the dissatisfaction may be very much like, i.e., negativism, complaints, deterioration of performance, and so forth. The improvement in the lighting of an employee's work area or raising his level of ay won't do much good if the source of the dissatisfaction is the absence of a meaningful assignment. By the same token, if an employee is dissatisfied with what he considers inequitable pay, the introduction of additional challenge in his work may simply make matters worse.

It is relatively easy for an employee to express frustration by complaining about pay, washroom conditions, fringe benefits, and so forth; but most people cannot easily express resentment in terms of the more abstract concepts concerning job growth, responsibility, and achievement.

It would be wrong to assume that there is no interaction between maintenance and motivational needs of employee. For example, conditions of high motivation often overshadow poor maintenance conditions. If an organization is in a period of strong growth and expansion, opportunities for job growth, responsibility, recognition, and achievement are usually abundant, but the rapid growth may have outrun the upkeep of maintenance factors. In this situation, motivation may be high, but only if employees recognize the poor maintenance conditions as unavoidable and temporary. The subordination of maintenance factors cannot go on indefinitely, even with the highest motivation.

Both maintenance and motivation factors influence the behavior of all employees, but employees are not identical and, furthermore, the needs of any individual do not remain orientation toward maintenance factors and those with greater sensitivity toward motivation factors.

A highly maintenance-oriented individual, preoccupied with the factors peripheral to his job rather than the job itself, is more concerned with comfort than challenge. He does not get deeply involved with his work but does with the condition of his work area, toilet facilities, and his time for going to lunch. By contrast, a strongly motivation-oriented employee is usually relatively indifferent to his surroundings and is caught up in the pursuit of work goals.

Fortunately, there are few people who are either exclusively maintenance-oriented or purely motivation-oriented. The former would be deadwood in an organization, while the latter might trample on those around him in his pursuit to achieve his goals.

6. With respect to employee motivational and maintenance needs, the management policies of an organization which is growing rapidly will probably result
   A. more in meeting motivational needs rather than maintenance needs
   B. more in meeting maintenance needs rather than motivational needs
   C. in meeting both of these needs equally
   D. in increased effort to define the motivational and maintenance needs of its employees

7. In accordance with the above passage, which of the following CANNOT be considered as an example of an employee maintenance need for railroad clerks?
   A. Providing more relief periods
   B. Providing fair salary increases at periodic intervals
   C. Increasing job responsibilities
   D. Increasing health insurance benefits

8. Most employees in an organization may be categorized as being interested in
   A. maintenance needs only
   B. motivational needs only
   C. both motivational and maintenance needs
   D. money only, to the exclusion of all other needs

Questions 9-11.

DIRECTIONS: Questions 9 through 11 are to be answered SOLELY on the basis of the following passage.

GOOD EMPLOYEE PRACTICES

As a city employee, you will be expected to take an interest in you work and perform the duties of your job to the best of your ability and in a spirit of cooperation. Nothing shows an interest in your work more than coming to work on time, not only at the start of the day but also when returning from lunch. If it is necessary for you to keep a personal appointment at lunch hour which might cause a delay in getting back to work on time, you should explain the situation to your supervisor and get his approval to come back a little late before you leave for lunch.

You should do everything that is asked of you willingly and consider important even the small jobs that your supervisor gives you. Although these jobs may seem unimportant, if you forget to do them or if you don't do them right, trouble may develop later.

Getting along well with your fellow workers will add much to the enjoyment of your work. You should respect your fellow workers and try to see their side when a disagreement arises. The better you get along with your fellow workers and your supervisor, the better you will like your job and the better you will be able to do it.

9. According to the above passage, in your job as a city employee, you are expected to
   A. show a willingness to cooperate on the job
   B. get your supervisor's approval before keeping any personal appointments at lunch hour
   C. avoid doing small jobs that seem unimportant
   D. do the easier jobs at the start of the day and the more difficult ones later on

10. According to the above passage, getting to work on time shows that you
    A. need the job
    B. have an interest in your work
    C. get along well with your fellow workers
    D. like your supervisor

11. According to the above passage, the one of the following statements that is NOT true is:
    A. If you do a small job wrong, trouble may develop
    B. You should respect your fellow workers
    C. If you disagree with a fellow worker, you should try to see his side of the story
    D. The less you get along with your supervisor, the better you will be able to do your job

Questions 12-15.

DIRECTIONS: Questions 12 through 15 are to be answered SOLELY on the basis of the following passage.

EMPLOYEE SUGGESTIONS

To increase the effectiveness of the city government, the city asks its employees to offer suggestions when they feel an improvement could be made in some government operation. The Employees' Suggestions Program was started to encourage city employees to do this. Through this Program, which is only for city employees, cash awards may be given to those whose suggestions are submitted and approved. Suggestions are looked for not only from supervisors but from all city employees as any city employee may get an idea which might be approved and contribute greatly to the solution of some problem of city government.

Therefore, all suggestions for improvement are welcome, whether they be suggestions on how to improve working conditions, or on how to increase the speed with which work is done, or on how to reduce or eliminate such things as waste, time losses, accidents or fire hazards. There are, however, a few types of suggestions for which cash awards cannot be given. An example of this type would be a suggestion to increase salaries or a suggestion to change the regulations about annual leave or about sick leave. The number of suggestions sent in has increased sharply during the past few years. It is hoped that it will keep increasing in the future in order to meet the city's needs for more ideas for improved ways of doing things.

12. According to the above passage, the MAIN reason why the city asks its employees for suggestions about government operations is to
    A. increase the effectiveness of the city government
    B. show that the Employees' Suggestion Program is working well
    C. show that everybody helps run the city government
    D. have the employee win a prize

    12.____

13. According to the above passage, the Employees' Suggestion Program can approve awards ONLY for those suggestions that come from
    A. city employees
    B. city employees who are supervisors
    C. city employees who are not supervisors
    D. experienced employee of the city

    13.____

14. According to the above passage, a cash award cannot be given through the Employees' Suggestion Program for a suggestion about
    A. getting work done faster
    B. helping prevent accidents on the job
    C. increasing the amount of annual leave for city employees
    D. reducing the chance of fire where city employees work

    14.____

15. According to the above passage, the suggestions sent in during the past few years have
    A. all been approved
    B. generally been well written
    C. been mostly about reducing or eliminating waste
    D. been greater in number than before

Questions 16-18.

DIRECTIONS: Questions 16 through 18 are to be answered SOLELY on the basis of the following passage.

The supervisor will gain the respect of the members of his staff and increase his influence over them by controlling his temper and avoiding criticizing anyone publicly. When a mistake is made, the good supervisor will take it over with the employee quietly and privately. The supervisor will listen to the employee's story, suggest the better way of doing the job, and offer help so the mistake won't happen again. Before closing the discussion, the supervisor should try to find something good to say about other parts of the employee's work. Some praise and appreciation, along with instruction, is more likely to encourage an employee to improve in those areas where he is weakest.

16. A good title that would show the meaning of the above passage would be
    A. How to Correct Employee Errors
    B. How to Praise Employees
    C. Mistakes are Preventable
    D. The Weak Employee

17. According to the above passage, the work of an employee who has made a mistake is more likely to improve if the supervisor
    A. avoids criticizing him
    B. gives him a chance to suggest a better way of doing the work
    C. listens to the employee's excuses to see if he is right
    D. praises good work at the same time he corrects the mistake

18. According to the above passage, when a supervisor needs to correct an employee's mistake, it is important that he
    A. allow some time to go by after the mistake is made
    B. do so when other employee are not present
    C. show his influence with his tone of voice
    D. tell other employee to avoid the same mistake

Questions 19-23.

DIRECTIONS: Questions 19 through 23 are to be answered SOLELY on the basis of the following passage.

In studying the relationships of people to the organizational structure, it is absolutely necessary to identify and recognize the informal organizational structure. These relationships are necessary when coordination of a plan is attempted. They may be with *the boss*, line supervisors, staff personnel, or other representatives of the formal organization's hierarchy, and they may include the *liaison men* who serve as the leaders of the informal organization. An acquaintanceship with the people serving in these roles in the organization, and its formal counterpart, permits a supervisor to recognize sensitive areas in which it is simple to get conflict reaction. Avoidance of such areas, plus conscious efforts to inform other people of his own objectives for various plans, will usually enlist their aid and support. Planning *without* people can lead to disaster because the individuals who must act together to make any plan a success are more important than the plans themselves.

19. Of the following titles, the one that MOST clearly describes the above passage is
    A. Coordination of a Function
    B. Avoidance of Conflict
    C. Planning With People
    D. Planning Objectives

20. According to the above passage, attempts at coordinating plans may fail unless
    A. the plan's objectives are clearly set forth
    B. conflict between groups is resolved
    C. the plans themselves are worthwhile
    D. informal relationships are recognized

21. According to the above passage, conflict
    A. may, in some cases, be desirable to secure results
    B. produces more heat than light
    C. should be avoided at all costs
    D. possibilities can be predicted by a sensitive supervisor

22. The above passage implies that
    A. informal relationships are more important than formal structure
    B. the weakness of a formal structure depends upon informal relationships
    C. liaison men are the key people to consult when taking formal and informal structures into account
    D. individuals in a group are at least as important as the plans for the group

23. The above passage suggests that
    A. some planning can be disastrous
    B. certain people in sensitive areas should be avoided
    C. the supervisor should discourage acquaintanceships in the organization
    D. organizational relationships should be consciously limited

Questions 24-25.

DIRECTIONS: Questions 24 and 25 are to be answered SOLELY on the basis of the following passage.

Good personnel relations of an organization depend upon mutual confidence, trust, and good will. The basis of confidence is understanding. Most troubles start with people who do not understand each other. When the organization's intentions or motives are misunderstood, or when reasons for actions, practices, or policies are misconstrued, complete cooperation from individuals is not forthcoming. If management expects full cooperation from employees, it has a responsibility of sharing with them the information which is the foundation of proper understanding, confidence, and trust. Personnel management has long since outgrown the days when it was the vogue to *treat them rough and tell them nothing*. Up-to-date personnel management provides all possible information about the activities, aims, and purposes of the organization. It seems altogether creditable that a desire should exist among employees for such information which the best-intentioned executive might think would not interest them and which the worst-intentioned would think was none of their business.

24. The above passage implies that one of the causes of the difficulty which an organization might have with its personnel relations is that its employees
    A. have not expressed interest in the activities, aims, and purposes of the organization
    B. do not believe in the good faith of the organization
    C. have not been able to give full cooperation to the organization
    D. do not recommend improvements in the practices and policies of the organization

25. According to the above passage, in order for an organization to have good personnel relations, it is NOT essential that
    A. employees have confidence in the organization
    B. the purposes of the organization be understood by the employees
    C. employees have a desire for information about the organization
    D. information about the organization be communicated to employees

KEY (CORRECT ANSWERS)

1.	D		11.	D
2.	C		12.	A
3.	D		13.	A
4.	B		14.	C
5.	A		15.	D
6.	A		16.	A
7.	C		17.	D
8.	C		18.	B
9.	A		19.	C
10.	B		20.	D

21. D
22. D
23. A
24. B
25. C

TEST 2

DIRECTIONS: Each question or incomplete statement is followed by several suggested answers or completions. Select the one that BEST answers the question or completes the statement. *PRINT THE LETTER OF THE CORRECT ANSWER IN THE SPACE AT THE RIGHT.*

Questions 1-8.

DIRECTIONS: Questions 1 through 8 are to be answered SOLELY on the basis of the following passage.

Important figures in education and in public affairs have recommended development of a private organization sponsored in part by various private foundations which would offer installment payment plans to full-time matriculated students in accredited colleges and universities in the United States and Canada. Contracts would be drawn to cover either tuition and fees, or tuition, fees, room and board in college facilities, from one year up to and including six years. A special charge, which would vary with the length of the contract, would be added to the gross repayable amount. This would be in addition to interest at a rate which would vary with the income of the parents. There would be a 3% annual interest charge for families with total income, before income taxes, of $50,000 or less. The rate would increase by 1/10 of 1% for every $1,000 of additional net income in excess of $50,000 up to a maximum of 10% interest. Contracts would carry an insurance provision on the life of the parent or guardian who signs the contract; all contracts must have the signature of a parent or guardian. Payment would be scheduled in equal monthly installments.

1. Which of the following students would be eligible for the payment plan described in the above passage? A
    A. matriculated student taking six semester hours toward a graduate degree
    B. matriculated student taking seventeen semester hours toward an undergraduate degree
    C. graduate matriculated at the University of Mexico taking eighteen semester hours toward a graduate degree
    D. student taking eighteen semester hours in a special pre-matriculation program

1.____

2. According to the above passage, the organization described would be sponsored in part by
    A. private foundations   B. colleges and universities
    C. persons in the field of education   D. persons in public life

2.____

3. Which of the following expenses could NOT be covered by a contract with the organization described in the above passage?
    A. Tuition amounting to $20,000 per year
    B. Registration and laboratory fees
    C. Meals at restaurants near the college
    D. Rent for an apartment in a college dormitory

3.____

4. The total amount to be paid would include ONLY the 4._____
   A. principal
   B. principal and interest
   C. principal, interest, and special charge
   D. principal, interest, special charge, and fee

5. The contract would carry insurance on the 5._____
   A. life of the student
   B. life of the student's parents
   C. income of the parents of the student
   D. life of the parent who signed the contract

6. The interest rate for an annual loan of $25,000 from the organization described in the above passage for a student whose family's net income was $55,000 should be 6._____
   A. 3%   B. 3.5%   C. 4%   D. 4.5%

7. The interest rate for an annual loan of $35,000 from the organization described in the above passage for a student whose family's net income was $100,000 should be 7._____
   A. 5%   B. 8%   C. 9%   D. 10%

8. John Lee has submitted an application for the installment payment plan described in the above passage. John's mother and father have a store which grossed $500,000 last year, but the income which the family received from the store was $90,000 before taxes. They also had $5,000 income from stock dividends. They paid $10,000 in income taxes.
   The amount of income upon which the interest should be based is 8._____
   A. $85,000   B. $90,000   C. $95,000   D. $105,000

Questions 9-13.

DIRECTIONS: Questions 9 through 13 are to be answered SOLELY on the basis of the following passage.

Since the organization chart is pictorial in nature, there is a tendency for it to be drawn in an artistically balanced and appealing fashion, regardless of the realities of actual organizational structure. In addition to being subject to this distortion, there is the difficulty of communicating in any organization chart the relative importance or the relative size of various component parts of an organizational structure. Furthermore, because of the need for simplicity of design, an organization chart can never indicate the full extent of the interrelationships among the component parts of an organization.

These interrelationships are often just as vital as the specifications which an organization chart endeavors to indicate. Yet, if an organization chart were to be drawn with all the wide variety of criss-crossing communication and cooperation networks existent within a typical organization, the chart would probably be much more confusing than informative. It is also obvious that no organization chart as such can prove or disprove that the organizational structure it represents is effective in realizing the objectives of the organization. At best, an organization chart can only illustrate some of the various factors to be taken into consideration in understanding, devising, or altering organizational arrangements.

9. According to the above passage, an organization chart can be expected to portray the
    A. structure of the organization along somewhat ideal lines
    B. relative size of the organizational units quite accurately
    C. channels of information distribution within the organization graphically
    D. extent of the obligation of each unit to meet the organizational objectives

9.____

10. According to the above passage, those aspects of internal functioning which are NOT shown on an organization chart
    A. can be considered to have little practical application in the operations of the organization
    B. might well be considered to be as important as the structural relationships which a chart does present
    C. could be the cause of considerable confusion in the operations of an organization which is quite large
    D. would be most likely to provide the information needed to determine the overall effectiveness of an organization

10.____

11. In the above passage, the one of the following conditions which is NOT implied as being a defect of an organization chart is that an organization chart may
    A. present a picture of the organizational structure which is different from the structure that actually exists
    B. fail to indicate the comparative size of various organizational units
    C. be limited in its ability to convey some of the meaningful aspects of organizational relationships
    D. become less useful over a period of time during which the organizational facts which it illustrated have changed

11.____

12. The one of the following which is the MOST suitable title for the above passage is
    A. The Design and Construction of an Organization Chart
    B. The Informal Aspects of an Organization Chart
    C. The Inherent Deficiencies of an Organization Chart
    D. The Utilization of a Typical Organization Chart

12.____

13. It can be inferred from the above passage that the function of an organization chart is to
    A. contribute to the comprehension of the organization form and arrangements
    B. establish the capabilities of the organization to operate effectively
    C. provide a balanced picture of the operations of the organization
    D. eliminate the need for complexity in the organization's structure

13.____

Questions 14-16.

DIRECTIONS: Questions 14 through 16 are to be answered SOLELY on the basis of the following passage.

In dealing with visitors to the school office, the school secretary must use initiative, tact, and good judgment. All visitors should be greeted promptly and courteously. The nature of their business should be determined quickly and handled expeditiously. Frequently, the secretary should be able to handle requests, deliveries, or passes herself. Her judgment should determine when a visitor should see members of the staff or the principal. Serious problems or doubtful cases should be referred to a supervisor.

14. In general, visitors should be handled by the 14.____
    A. school secretary   B. principal
    C. appropriate supervisor D. person who is free

15. It is wise to obtain the following information from visitors: 15.____
    A. Name   B. Nature of business
    C. Address D. Problems they have

16. All visitors who wish to see members of the staff should 16.____
    A. be permitted to do so   B. produce identification
    C. do so for valid reasons only D. be processed by a supervisor

Questions 17-19.

DIRECTIONS: Questions 17 through 19 are to be answered SOLELY on the basis of the following passage.

Information regarding payroll status, salary differentials, promotional salary increments, deductions, and pension payments should be given to all members of the staff who have questions regarding these items. On occasion, if the secretary is uncertain regarding the information, the staff member should be referred to the principal or the appropriate agency. No question by a staff member regarding payroll status should be brushed aside as immaterial or irrelevant. The school secretary must always try to handle the question or pass it on to the person who can handle it.

17. If a teacher is dissatisfied with information regarding her salary status, as given 17.____
    by the school secretary, the matter should be
    A. dropped
    B. passed on to the principal
    C. passed on by the secretary to proper agency or the principal
    D. made a basis for grievance procedures

18. The following is an adequate summary of the above passage: 18.____
    A. The secretary must handle all payroll matters
    B. The secretary must handle all payroll matter or know who can handle them
    C. The secretary or the principal must handle all payroll matters
    D. Payroll matter too difficult to handle must be followed up until they are solved

19. The above passage implies that   19._____
    A. many teachers ask immaterial questions regarding payroll status
    B. few teachers ask irrelevant pension questions
    C. no teachers ask immaterial salary questions
    D. no question regarding salary should be considered irrelevant

Questions 20-22.

DIRECTIONS: Questions 20 through 22 are to be answered SOLELY on the basis of the following passage.

The necessity for good speech on the part of the school secretary cannot be overstated. The school secretary must deal with the general public, the pupils, the members of the staff, and the school supervisors. In every situation which involves the general public, the secretary serves as a representative of the school. In dealing with pupils, the secretary's speech must serve as a model from which students may guide themselves. Slang, colloquialisms, malapropisms, and local dialects must be avoided.

20. The above passage implies that the speech pattern of the secretary must be   20._____
    A. perfect   B. very good
    C. average   D. on a level with that of the pupils

21. The last sentence indicates that slang   21._____
    A. is acceptable   B. occurs in all speech
    C. might be used occasionally D. should be shunned

22. The above passage implies that the speech of pupils   22._____
    A. may be influenced   B. does not change readily
    C. is generally good   D. is generally poor

Questions 23-25.

DIRECTIONS: Questions 23 through 25 are to be answered SOLELY on the basis of the following passage.

The school secretary who is engaged in the task of filing records and correspondence should follow a general set of rules. Items which are filed should be available to other secretaries or to supervisors quickly and easily by means of the application of a modicum of common sense and good judgment. Items which, by their nature, may be difficult to find should be cross-indexed. Folders and drawers should be neatly and accurately labeled. There should never be a large accumulation of papers which have not been filed.

23. A good general rule to follow in filing is that materials should be   23._____
    A. placed in folders quickly   B. neatly stored
    C. readily available   D. cross-indexed

24. Items that are filed should be available to
    A. the secretary charged with the task of filing
    B. secretaries and supervisors
    C. school personnel
    D. the principal

24.____

25. A modicum of common sense means _____ common sense.
    A. an average amount of   B. a great deal of
    C. a little   D. no

25.____

KEY (CORRECT ANSWERS)

1.	B		11.	D
2.	A		12.	C
3.	C		13.	A
4.	C		14.	A
5.	D		15.	B
6.	B		16.	C
7.	B		17.	C
8.	C		18.	B
9.	A		19.	D
10.	B		20.	B

21. D
22. A
23. C
24. B
25. C

TEST 3

DIRECTIONS: Each question or incomplete statement is followed by several suggested answers or completions. Select the one that BEST answers the question or completes the statement. *PRINT THE LETTER OF THE CORRECT ANSWER IN THE SPACE AT THE RIGHT.*

Questions 1-4.

DIRECTIONS: Questions 1 through 4 are to be answered SOLELY on the basis of the following passage.

    The proposition that administrative activity is essentially the same in all organizations appears to underlie some of the practices in the administration of private higher education. Although the practice is unusual in public education, there are numerous instances of industrial, governmental, or military administrators being assigned to private institutions of higher education and, to a lesser extent, of college and university presidents assuming administrative positions in other types of organizations. To test this theory that administrators are interchangeable, there is a need for systematic observation and classification. The myth that an educational administrator must first have experience in the teaching profession is firmly rooted in a long tradition that has historical prestige. The myth is bound up in the expectations of the public and personnel surrounding the administrator. Since administrative success depends significantly on how well an administrator meets the expectations others have of him, the myth may be more powerful than the special experience in helping the administrator attain organizational and educational objectives. Educational administrators who have risen through the teaching profession have often expressed nostalgia for the life of a teacher or scholar, but there is no evidence that this nostalgia contributes to administrative success.

1. Which of the following statements as completed is MOST consistent with the above passage?
The greatest number of administrators has moved from
   A. industry and the military to government and universities
   B. government and universities to industry and the military
   C. government, the armed forces, and industry to colleges and universities
   D. colleges and universities to government, the armed forces, and industry

1.____

2. Of the following, the MOST reasonable inference from the above passage is that a specific area requiring further research is the
   A. place of myth in the tradition and history of the educational profession
   B. relative effectiveness of educational administrators from inside and outside the teaching profession
   C. performance of administrators in the administration of public colleges
   D. degree of reality behind the nostalgia for scholarly pursuits often expressed by educational administrators

2.____

3. According to the above passage, the value to an educational administrator of experience in the teaching profession
   A. lies in the first-hand knowledge he has acquired of immediate educational problems
   B. may lie in the belief of his colleagues, subordinates, and the public that such experience is necessary
   C. has been supported by evidence that the experience contributes to administrative success in educational fields
   D. would be greater if the administrator were able to free himself from nostalgia for his former duties

3.____

4. Of the following, the MOST suitable title for the above passage is
   A. Educational Administration, Its Problems
   B. The Experience Needed For Educational Administration
   C. Administration in Higher Education
   D. Evaluating Administrative Experience

4.____

Questions 5-6.

DIRECTIONS: Questions 5 and 6 are to be answered SOLELY on the basis of the following passage.

Management by objectives (MBO) may be defined as the process by which the superior and the subordinate managers of an organization jointly define its common goals, define each individual's major areas of responsibility in terms of the results expected of him and use these measure as guides for operating the unit and assessing the contribution of each of its members.

The MBO approach requires that after organizational goals are established and communicated, targets must be set for each individual position which are congruent with organizational goals. Periodic performance reviews and a final review using the objectives set as criteria are also basic to this approach.

Recent studies have shown that MBO programs are influenced by attitudes and perceptions of the boss, the company, the reward-punishment system, and the program itself. In addition, the manner in which the MBO program is carried out can influence the success of the program. A study done in the late sixties indicates that the best results are obtained when the manager sets goals which deal with significant problem areas in the organizational unit, or with the subordinate's personal deficiencies. These goals must be clear with regard to what is expected of the subordinate. The frequency of feedback is also important in the success of a management-by-objectives program. Generally, the greater the amount of feedback, the more successful the MBO program.

5. According to the above passage, the expected output for individual employees should be determined
   A. after a number of reviews of work performance
   B. after common organizational goals are defined
   C. before common organizational goals are defined
   D. on the basis of an employee's personal qualities

5.____

6. According to the above passage, the management-by-objectives approach requires
   A. less feedback than other types of management programs
   B. little review of on-the-job performance after the initial setting of goals
   C. general conformance between individual goals and organizational goals
   D. the setting of goals which deal with minor problem areas in the organization

6.____

Questions 7-10.

DIRECTIONS: Questions 7 through 10 are to be answered SOLELY on the basis of the following passage.

Management, which is the function of executive leadership, has as its principal phases the planning, organizing, and controlling of the activities of subordinate groups in the accomplishment of organizational objectives. Planning specifies the kind and extent of the factors, forces, and effects, and the relationships among them, that will be required for satisfactory accomplishment. The nature of the objectives and their requirements must be known before determinations can be made as to what must be done, how it must be done and why, where actions should take place, who should be responsible, and similar programs pertaining to the formulation of a plan. Organizing, which creates the conditions that must be present before the execution of the plan can be undertaken successfully, cannot be done intelligently without knowledge of the organizational objectives. Control, which has to do with the constraint and regulation of activities entering into the execution of the plan, must be exercised in accordance with the characteristics and requirements of the activities demanded by the plan.

7. The one of the following which is the MOST suitable title for the above passage is
   A. The Nature of Successful Organization
   B. The Planning of Management Functions
   C. The Importance of Organizational Functions
   D. The Principle Aspects of Management

7.____

8. It can be inferred from the above passage that the one of the following functions whose existence is essential to the existence of the other three is the
   A. regulation of the work needed to carry out a plan
   B. understanding of what the organization intends to accomplish
   C. securing of information of the factors necessary for accomplishment of objectives
   D. establishment of the conditions required for successful action

8.____

9. The one of the following which would NOT be included within any of the principal phases of the function of executive leadership as defined in the above passage is
   A. determination of manpower requirements
   B. procurement of required material
   C. establishment of organizational objectives
   D. scheduling of production

9.____

10. The conclusion which can MOST reasonably be drawn from the above passage is that the control phase of managing is most directly concerned with the   10.____
    A. influencing of policy determinations
    B. administering of suggestion systems
    C. acquisition of staff for the organization
    D. implementation of performance standards

Questions 11-12.

DIRECTIONS: Questions 11 and 12 are to be answered SOLELY on the basis of the following passage.

Under an open-and-above-board policy, it is to be expected that some supervisors will gloss over known shortcomings of subordinates rather than face the task of discussing team face-to-face. It is also to be expected that at least some employees whose job performance is below par will reject the supervisor's appraisal as biased and unfair. Be that as it may, these are inescapable aspects of any performance appraisal system in which human beings are involved. The supervisor who shies away from calling a spade a spade, as well as the employee with a chip on his shoulder, will each in his own way eventually be revealed in his true light—to the benefit of the organization as a whole.

11. The BEST of the following interpretations of the above passage is that   11.____
    A. the method of rating employee performance requires immediate revision to improve employee acceptance
    B. substandard performance ratings should be discussed with employees even if satisfactory ratings are not
    C. supervisors run the risk of being called unfair by the subordinates even though their appraisals are accurate
    D. any system of employee performance rating is satisfactory if used properly

12. The BEST of the following interpretations of the above passage is that   12.____
    A. supervisors generally are not open-and-above-board with their subordinates
    B. it is necessary for supervisors to tell employees objectively how they are performing
    C. employees complain when their supervisor does not keep them informed
    D. supervisors are afraid to tell subordinates their weaknesses

Questions 13-15.

DIRECTIONS: Questions 13 through 15 are to be answered SOLELY on the basis of the following passage.

During the last decade, a great deal of interest has been generated around the phenomenon of *organizational development,* or the process of developing human resources through conscious organization effort. Organizational development (OD) stresses improving interpersonal relationships and organizational skills, such as communication, to a much greater degree than individual training ever did. The kind of training that an organization should emphasize depends upon the present and future structure of the organization. If future organizations are to be unstable, shifting coalitions, then individual skills and abilities, particularly those emphasizing innovativeness, creativity, flexibility, and the latest technological knowledge, are crucial and individual training is most appropriate.

But if there is to be little change in organizational structure, then the main thrust of training should be group-oriented or organizational development. This approach seems better designed for overcoming hierarchical barriers, for developing a degree of interpersonal relationships which make communication along the chain of command possible, and for retaining a modicum of innovation and/or flexibility.

13. According to the above passage, group-oriented training is MOST useful in in
    A. developing a communications system that will facilitate understanding through the chain of command
    B. highly flexible and mobile organizations
    C. preventing the crossing of hierarchical barriers within an organization
    D. saving energy otherwise wasted on developing methods of dealing with rigid hierarchies

14. The one of the following conclusions which can be drawn MOST appropriately from the above passage is that
    A. behavioral research supports the use of organizational development training methods rather than individualized training
    B. it is easier to provide individualized training in specific skills than to set up sensitivity training programs
    C. organizational development eliminates innovative or flexible activity
    D. the nature of an organization greatly influences which training methods will be most effective

15. According to the above passage, the one of the following which is LEAST important for large-scale organizations geared to rapid and abrupt change is
    A. current technological information
    B. development of a high degree of interpersonal relationships
    C. development of individual skills and abilities
    D. emphasis on creativity

Questions 16-18.

DIRECTIONS: Questions 16 through 18 are to be answered SOLELY on the basis of the following passage.

The increase in the extent to which each individual is personally responsible to others is most noticeable in a large bureaucracy. No one person *decides* anything; each decision of any importance, is the product of an intricate process of brokerage involving individuals inside and outside the organization who feel some reason to be affected by the decision, or two have special knowledge to contribute to it. The more varied the organization's constituency, the more inside *veto-groups* will need to be taken into account. But even if no outside consultations were involved, sheer size would produce a complex process of decision. For a large organization is a deliberately created system of tensions into which each individual is expected to bring workways, viewpoints, and outside relationships markedly different from those of his colleagues. It is the administrator's task to draw from these disparate forces the elements of wise action from day to day, consistent with the purposes of the organization as a whole.

16. The above passage is essentially a description of decision-making as 16.____
    A. an organization process
    B. the key responsibility of the administrator
    C. the one best position among many
    D. a complex of individual decisions

17. Which one of the following statements BEST describes the responsibilities of an administrator? 17.____
    A. He modifies decisions and goals in accordance with pressures from within and outside the organization.
    B. He creates problem-solving mechanisms that rely on the varied interests of his staff and *veto-groups*.
    C. He makes determinations that will lead to attainment of his agency's objectives.
    D. He obtains agreement among varying viewpoints and interests

18. In the context of the operations of a central public personnel agency, a *veto-group* would LEAST likely consist of 18.____
    A. employee organizations
    B. professional personnel societies
    C. using agencies
    D. civil service newspapers

Questions 19-25.

DIRECTIONS: Questions 19 through 25 are to be answered SOLELY on the basis of the following passage, which is an extract from a report prepared for Department X, which outlines the procedure to be followed in the case of transfers of employees.

Every transfer, regardless of the reason therefore, requires completion of the record of transfer, Form DT411. To denote consent to the transfer, DT411 should contain the signatures of the transferee and the personnel officer(s) concerned, except that, in the case of an involuntary transfer, the signatures of the transferee's present and prospective supervisors shall be entered in Boxes 8A and 8B, respectively, since the transferee does not consent. Only a permanent employee may request a transfer; in such cases, the employee's attendance record shall be duly considered with regard to absences, latenesses, and accrued overtime balances. In the case of an inter-district transfer, the employee's attendance record must be included in Section 8A of the transfer request, Form DT410, by the personnel officer of the district from which the transfer is requested. The personnel officer of the district to which the employee requested transfer may refuse to accept accrued overtime balances in excess of ten days.

An employee on probation shall be eligible for transfer. If such employee is involuntarily transferred, he shall be credited for the period of time already served on probation. However, if such transfer is voluntary, the employee shall be required to serve the entire period of his probation in the new position. An employee who has occurred a disability which prevents him from performing his normal duties may be transferred during the period of such disability to other appropriate duties. A disability transfer requires the completion of either DT414 if the disability is job-connected, or Form DT415 if it is not a job-connected disability. In either case, the personnel officer of the district from which the transfer is made signs in Box 6A of the first two copies and the personnel officer of the district to which the transfer is made signs in Box 6B of the last two copies, or, in the case of an intra-district disability transfer, the personnel officer must sign in Box 6A of the first two copies and Box 6B of the last two copies.

19. When a personnel officer consents to an employee's request for transfer from his district, this procedure requires that the personnel officer sign Forms
    A. DT411
    B. DT410 and DT411
    C. DT411 and either Form DT414 or DT415
    D. DT410 and DT411, and either Form DT414 or DT415

20. With respect to the time record of an employee transferred against his wishes during his probationary period, this procedure requires that
    A. he serve the entire period of his probation in his present office
    B. he lose his accrued overtime balance
    C. his attendance record be considered with regard to absences and latenesses
    D. he be given credit for the period of time he has already served on probation

21. Assume you are a supervisor and an employee must be transferred into your office against his wishes.
    According to this procedure, the box you must sign on the record of transfer is
    A. 6A   B. 8A   C. 6B   D. 8B

22. Under this procedure, in the case of a disability transfer, when must Box 6A on Forms DT414 and DT415 be signed by the personnel officer of the district to which the transfer is being made?
    A. In all cases when either Form DT414 or Form DT415 is used
    B. In all cases when Form DT414 is used and only under certain circumstances when Form DT415 is used
    C. In all cases when Form DT415 is used and only under certain circumstances when Form DT414 is used
    D. Only under certain circumstances when either Form DT414 or Form DT415 is used

23. From the above passage, it may be inferred MOST correctly that the number of copies of Form DT414 is
    A. no more than 2
    B. at least 3
    C. at least 5
    D. more than the number of copies of Form DT415

24. A change in punctuation and capitalization only which would change one sentence into two and possibly contribute to somewhat greater ease of reading this report extract would be MOST appropriate in the
    A. 2nd sentence, 1st paragraph
    B. 3rd sentence, 1st paragraph
    C. next to the last sentence, 2nd paragraph
    D. 2nd sentence, 2nd paragraph

25. In the second paragraph, a word that is INCORRECTLY used is
    A. *shall* in the 1st sentence
    B. *voluntary* in the 3rd sentence
    C. *occurred* in the 4th sentence
    D. *intra-district* in the last sentence

KEY (CORRECT ANSWERS)

1.	C		11.	C
2.	B		12.	B
3.	B		13.	A
4.	B		14.	D
5.	B		15.	B
6.	C		16.	A
7.	D		17.	C
8.	B		18.	B
9.	C		19.	A
10.	D		20.	D

21. D
22. D
23. B
24. B
25. C

INTERPRETING STATISTICAL DATA GRAPHS, CHARTS AND TABLES
EXAMINATION SECTION
TEST 1

DIRECTIONS: Each question or incomplete statement is followed by several suggested answers or completions. Select the one that BEST answers the question or completes the statement. *PRINT THE LETTER OF THE CORRECT ANSWER IN THE SPACE AT THE RIGHT.*

Questions 1-3.

DIRECTIONS: Questions 1 through 3 are to be answered SOLELY on the basis of the following table.

QUARTERLY SALES REPORTED BY MAJOR INDUSTRY GROUPS
DECEMBER 2011 - FEBRUARY 2013
Reported Sales, Taxable & Non-Taxable
(In Millions)

Industry Groups	12/11-2/12	3/12-5/12	6/12-8/12	9/12-11/12	12/12-2/13
Retailers	2,802	2,711	2,475	2,793	2,974
Wholesalers	2,404	2,237	2,269	2,485	2,512
Manufacturers	3,016	2,888	3,001	3,518	3,293
Services	1,034	1,065	984	1,132	1,092

1. The trend in total reported sales may be described as
    A. downward
    B. downward and upward
    C. horizontal
    D. upward

2. The two industry groups that reveal a similar seasonal pattern for the period December 2011 through November 2012 are
    A. retailers and manufacturers
    B. retailers and wholesalers
    C. wholesalers and manufacturers
    D. wholesalers and service

3. Reported sales were at a MINIMUM between
    A. December 2011 and February 2012
    B. March 2012 and May 2012
    C. June 2012 and August 2012
    D. September 2012 and November 2012

TEST 2

DIRECTIONS: Each question or incomplete statement is followed by several suggested answers or completions. Select the one that BEST answers the question or completes the statement. *PRINT THE LETTER OF THE CORRECT ANSWER IN THE SPACE AT THE RIGHT.*

Questions 1-4.

DIRECTIONS: Questions 1 through 4 are to be answered SOLELY on the basis of the following information.

The income elasticity of demand for selected items of consumer demand in the United States are:

Item	Elasticity
Airline Travel	5.66
Alcohol	.62
Dentist Fees	1.00
Electric Utilities	3.00
Gasoline	1.29
Intercity Bus	1.89
Local Bus	1.41
Restaurant Meals	.75

1. The demand for the item listed below that would be MOST adversely affected by a decrease in income is

   A. alcohol
   B. electric utilities
   C. gasoline
   D. restaurant meals

2. The item whose relative change in demand would be the same as the relative change in income would be

   A. dentist fees
   B. gasoline
   C. restaurant meals
   D. none of the above

3. If income increases by 12 percent, the demand for restaurant meals may be expected to increase by

   A. 9 percent
   B. 12 percent
   C. 16 percent
   D. none of the above

4. On the basis of the above information, the item whose demand would be MOST adversely affected by an increase in the sales tax from 7 percent to 8 percent to be passed on to the consumer in the form of higher prices

   A. would be airline travel
   B. would be alcohol
   C. would be gasoline
   D. cannot be determined

TEST 3

DIRECTIONS: Each question or incomplete statement is followed by several suggested answers or completions. Select the one that BEST answers the question or completes the statement. *PRINT THE LETTER OF THE CORRECT ANSWER IN THE SPACE AT THE RIGHT.*

Questions 1-3.

DIRECTIONS: Questions 1 through 3 are to be answered SOLELY on the basis of the following graphs depicting various relationships in a single retail store.

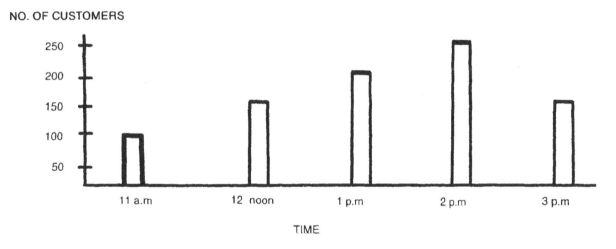

GRAPH I
RELATIONSHIP BETWEEN NUMBER OF CUSTOMERS
STORE AND TIME OF DAY

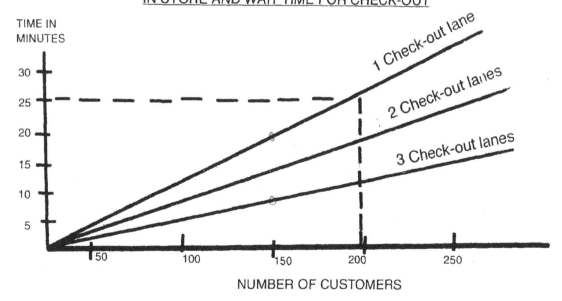

GRAPH II
RELATIONSHIP BETWEEN NUMBER OF CHECK-OUT LANES AVAILABLE
IN STORE AND WAIT TIME FOR CHECK-OUT

Note the dotted lines in Graph II. They demonstrate that, if there are 200 people in the store and only 1 check-out lane is open, the wait time will be 25 minutes.

1. At what time would a person be most likely NOT to have to wait more than 15 minutes if only one check-out lane is open?

   A. 11 A.M.   B. 12 Noon   C. 1 P.M.   D. 3 P.M.

2. At what time of day would a person have to wait the LONGEST to check out if 3 check-out lanes are available?

   A. 11 A.M.   B. 12 Noon   C. 1 P.M.   D. 2 P.M.

3. The difference in wait times between 1 and 3 check-out lanes at 3 P.M. is MOST NEARLY

   A. 5   B. 10   C. 15   D. 20

TEST 4

DIRECTIONS: Each question or incomplete statement is followed by several suggested answers or completions. Select the one that BEST answers the question or completes the statement. *PRINT THE LETTER OF THE CORRECT ANSWER IN THE SPACE AT THE RIGHT.*

Questions 1-4.

DIRECTIONS: Questions 1 through 4 are to be answered SOLELY on the basis of the graph below.

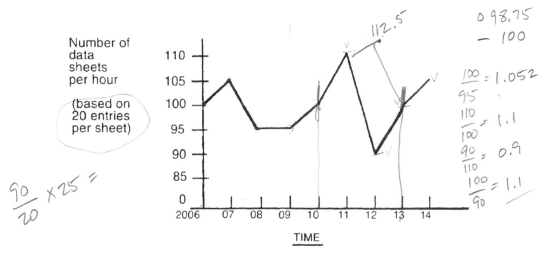

1. Of the following, during what four-year period did the average output of computer operators fall BELOW 100 sheets per hour? 1.____

    A. 2007-10   B. 2008-11   C. 2010-13   D. 2011-14

2. The average percentage change in output over the previous year's output for the years 2009 to 2012 is MOST NEARLY 2.____

    A. 2   B. 0   C. -5   D. -7

3. The difference between the actual output for 2002 and the projected figure based upon the average increase from 2006-2011 is MOST NEARLY 3.____

    A. 18   B. 20   C. 22   D. 24

4. Assume that after constructing the above graph you, an analyst, discovered that the average number of entries per sheet in 2012 was 25 (instead of 20) because of the complex nature of the work performed during that period. 4.____
The average output in cards per hour for the period 2010-13, expressed in terms of 20 items per sheet, would then be MOST NEARLY

    A. 95   B. 100   C. 105   D. 110

TEST 5

DIRECTIONS: Each question or incomplete statement is followed by several suggested answers or completions. Select the one that BEST answers the question or completes the statement. *PRINT THE LETTER OF THE CORRECT ANSWER IN THE SPACE AT THE RIGHT.*

Questions 1-3.

DIRECTIONS: Questions 1 through 3 are to be answered on the basis of the following data assembled for a cost-benefit analysis.

	Cost	Benefit
No program	0	0
Alternative W	$ 3,000	$ 6,000
Alternative X	$10,000	$17,000
Alternative Y	$17,000	$25,000
Alternative Z	$30,000	$32,000

1. From the point of view of selecting the alternative with the best cost benefit ratio, the BEST alternative is Alternative   1.____

   A. W   B. X   C. Y   D. Z

2. From the point of view of selecting the alternative with the best measure of net benefit, the BEST alternative is Alternative   2.____

   A. W   B. X   C. Y   D. Z

3. From the point of view of pushing public expenditure to the point where marginal benefit equals or exceeds marginal cost, the BEST alternative is Alternative   3.____

   A. W   B. X   C. Y   D. Z

TEST 6

DIRECTIONS: Each question or incomplete statement is followed by several suggested answers or completions. Select the one that BEST answers the question or completes the statement. *PRINT THE LETTER OF THE CORRECT ANSWER IN THE SPACE AT THE RIGHT.*

Questions 1-3.

DIRECTIONS: Questions 1 through 3 are to be answered SOLELY on the basis of the following data.

A series of cost-benefit studies of various alternative health programs yields the following results:

Program	Benefit	Cost
K	30	15
L	60	60
M	300	150
N	600	500

In answering Questions 1 and 2, assume that all programs can be increased or decreased in scale without affecting their individual benefit-to-cost ratios.

1. The benefit-to-cost ratio of Program M is

   A. 10:1   B. 5:1   C. 2:1   D. 1:2

   1.____

2. The budget ceiling for one or more of the programs included in the study is set at 75 units.
   It may MOST logically be concluded that

   A. Programs K and L should be chosen to fit within the budget ceiling
   B. Program K would be the most desirable one that could be afforded
   C. Program M should be chosen rather than Program K
   D. the choice should be between Programs M and K

   2.____

3. If no assumptions can be made regarding the effects of change of scale, the MOST logical conclusion, on the basis of the data available, is that

   A. more data are needed for a budget choice of program
   B. Program K is the most preferable because of its low cost and good benefit-to-cost ratio
   C. Program M is the most preferable because of its high benefits and good benefit-to-cost ratio
   D. there is no difference between Programs K and M, and either can be chosen for any purpose

   3.____

TEST 7

DIRECTIONS: Each question or incomplete statement is followed by several suggested answers or completions. Select the one that BEST answers the question or completes the statement. *PRINT THE LETTER OF THE CORRECT ANSWER IN THE SPACE AT THE RIGHT.*

Questions 1-6.

DIRECTIONS: Questions 1 through 6 are to be answered SOLELY on the basis of the information contained in the charts below which relate to the budget allocations of City X, a small suburban community. The charts depict the annual budget allocations by Department and by expenditures over a five-year period.

CITY X BUDGET IN MILLIONS OF DOLLARS

TABLE I. Budget Allocations By Department

Department	2007	2008	2009	2010	2011
Public Safety	30	45	50	40	50
Health and Welfare	50	75	90	60	70
Engineering	5	8	10	5	8
Human Resources	10	12	20	10	22
Conservation & Environment	10	15	20	20	15
Education & Development	15	25	35	15	15
TOTAL BUDGET	120	180	225	150	180

TABLE II. Budget Allocations by Expenditures

Category	2007	2008	2009	2010	2011
Raw Materials & Machinery	36	63	68	30	98
Capital Outlay	12	27	56	15	18
Personal Services	72	90	101	105	64
TOTAL BUDGET	120	180	225	150	180

1. The year in which the SMALLEST percentage of the total annual budget was allocated to the Department of Education and Development is

   A. 2007   B. 2008   C. 2010   D. 2011

2. Assume that in 2010 the Department of Conservation and Environment divided its annual budget into the three categories of expenditures and in exactly the same proportion as the budget shown in Table II for the year 2010. The amount allocated for capital outlay in the Department of Conservation and Environment's 2010 budget was MOST NEARLY _____ million.

   A. $2   B. $4   C. $6   D. $10

120

2 (#7)

3. From the year 2008 to the year 2010, the sum of the annual budgets for the Departments of Public Safety and Engineering showed an overall _____ million.

   A. decline; $8
   B. increase; $7
   C. decline; $15
   D. increase; $22

   3.____

4. The LARGEST dollar increase in departmental budget allocations from one year to the next was in _____ from _____.

   A. Public Safety; 2007 to 2008   15
   B. Health and Welfare; 2007 to 2008   25
   C. Education and Development; 2009 to 2010   -20
   D. Human Resources; 2009 to 2010

   4.____

5. During the five-year period, the annual budget of the Department of Human Resources was GREATER than the annual budget for the Department of Conservation and Environment in _____ of the years.

   A. none   B. one   C. two   D. three

   5.____

6. If the total City X budget increases at the same rate from 2011 to 2012 as it did from 2010 to 2011, the total City X budget for 2012 will be MOST NEARLY _____ million.

   A. $180   B. $200   C. $210   D. $215

   6.____

$\frac{180}{150} = 1.2$ $\frac{x}{180} = 1.2$

TEST 8

DIRECTIONS: Each question or incomplete statement is followed by several suggested answers or completions. Select the one that BEST answers the question or completes the statement. *PRINT THE LETTER OF THE CORRECT ANSWER IN THE SPACE AT THE RIGHT.*

Questions 1-3.

DIRECTIONS: Questions 1 through 3 are to be answered SOLELY on the basis of the following information.

Assume that in order to encourage Program A, the State and Federal governments have agreed to make the following reimbursements for money spent on Program A, provided the unreimbursed balance is paid from City funds.

During Fiscal Year 2011-2012 - For the first $2 million expended, 50% Federal reimbursement and 30% State reimbursement; for the next $3 million, 40% Federal reimbursement and 20% State reimbursement; for the next $5 million, 20% Federal reimbursement and 10% State reimbursement. Above $10 million expended, no Federal or State reimbursement.

During Fiscal Year 2012-2013 - For the first $1 million expended, 30% Federal reimbursement and 20% State reimbursement; for the next $4 million, 15% Federal reimbursement and 10% State reimbursement. Above $5 million expended, no Federal or State reimbursement.

1. Assume that the Program A expenditures are such that the State reimbursement for Fiscal Year 2011-2012 will be $1 million.
   Then, the Federal reimbursement for Fiscal Year 2011-2012 will be

   A. $1,600,000   B. $1,800,000
   C. $2,000,000   D. $2,600,000

2. Assume that $8 million were to be spent on Program A in Fiscal Year 2012-2013.
   The TOTAL amount of unreimbursed City funds required would be

   A. $3,500,000   B. $4,500,000
   C. $5,500,000   D. $6,500,000

3. Assume that the City desires to have a combined total of $6 million spent in Program A during both the Fiscal Year 2011-2012 and the Fiscal Year 2012-2013.
   Of the following expenditure combinations, the one which results in the GREATEST reimbursement of City funds is _____ in Fiscal Year 2011-2012 and _____ in Fiscal Year 2012-2013.

   A. $5 million; $1 million   B. $4 million; $2 million
   C. $3 million; $3 million   D. $2 million; $4 million

KEY (CORRECT ANSWERS)

TEST 1	TEST 2	TEST 3	TEST 4
1. D	1. B	1. A	1. A
2. C	2. A	2. D	2. B
3. C	3. A	3. B	3. C
	4. D		4. C

TEST 5	TEST 6	TEST 7	TEST 8
1. A	1. C	1. D	1. B
2. C	2. D	2. A	2. D
3. C	3. A	3. A	3. A
		4. B	
		5. B	
		6. D	

---

		fed	state	city	
11-12	2m	1m	600k	400k	
	3m	1.2m	600k	1.2m	
	5m	1m	500k	350m	

12-13	1m	300k	200k	500k	500k + 3m (.25)
	4m	600k	400k	3m	
	3m	—	—	3m	

PREPARING WRITTEN MATERIAL

PARAGRAPH REARRANGEMENT
COMMENTARY

The sentences that follow are in scrambled order. You are to rearrange them in proper order and indicate the letter choice containing the correct answer at the space at the right.

Each group of sentences in this section is actually a paragraph presented in scrambled order. Each sentence in the group has a place in that paragraph; no sentence is to be left out. You are to read each group of sentences and decide upon the best order in which to put the sentences so as to form a well-organized paragraph.

The questions in this section measure the ability to solve a problem when all the facts relevant to its solution are not given.

More specifically, certain positions of responsibility and authority require the employee to discover connection between events sometimes, apparently, unrelated. In order to do this, the employee will find it necessary to correctly infer that unspecified events have probably occurred or are likely to occur. This ability becomes especially important when action must be taken on incomplete information.

Accordingly, these questions require competitors to choose among several suggested alternatives, each of which presents a different sequential arrangement of the events. Competitors must choose the MOST logical of the suggested sequences.

In order to do so, they may be required to draw on general knowledge to infer missing concepts or events that are essential to sequencing the given events. Competitors should be careful to infer only what is essential to the sequence. The plausibility of the wrong alternatives will always require the inclusion of unlikely events or of additional chains of events which are NOT essential to sequencing the given events.

It's very important to remember that you are looking for the best of the four possible choices, and that the best choice of all may not even be one of the answers you're given to choose from.

There is no one right way to solve these problems. Many people have found it helpful to first write out the order of the sentences, as they would have arranged them, on their scrap paper before looking at the possible answers. If their optimum answer is there, this can save them some time. If it isn't, this method can still give insight into solving the problem. Others find it most helpful to just go through each of the possible choices, contrasting each as they go along. You should use whatever method feels comfortable and works for you.

While most of these types of questions are not that difficult, we've added a higher percentage of the difficult type, just to give you more practice. Usually there are only one or two questions on this section that contain such subtle distinctions that you're unable to answer confidently. And you then may find yourself stuck deciding between two possible choices, neither of which you're sure about.

EXAMINATION SECTION

TEST 1

DIRECTIONS: The sentences that follow are in scrambled order. You are to rearrange them in proper order and indicate the letter choice containing the correct answer. *PRINT THE LETTER OF THE CORRECT ANSWER IN THE SPACE AT THE RIGHT.*

1. Below are four statements labeled W, X, Y and Z.
   W. He was a strict and fanatic drillmaster.
   X. The word is always used in a derogatory sense and generally shows resentment and anger on the part of the user.
   Y. It is from the name of this Frenchman that we derive our English word, martinet.
   Z. Jean Martinet was the Inspector-General of Infantry during the reign of King Louis XIV.
   The PROPER order in which these sentences should be placed in a paragraph is:
   A. X, Z, W, Y   B. X, Z, Y, W   C. Z, W, Y, X   D. Z, Y, W, X

   1.____

2. In the following paragraph, the sentences, which are numbered, have been jumbled.
   I. Since then it has undergone changes.
   II. It was incorporated in 1955 under the laws of the State of New York.
   III. Its primary purposes, a cleaner city, has, however, remained the same.
   IV. The Citizens Committee works in cooperation with the Mayor's Inter-departmental Committee for a Clean City.
   The order in which these sentences should be arranged to form a well-organized paragraph is:
   A. II, IV, I, III   B. III, IV, I, II   C. IV, II, I, III   D. IV, III, II, I

   2.____

   3.____

Questions 3-5.

DIRECTIONS: The sentences listed below are part of a meaningful paragraph but they are not given in their proper order. You are to decide what would be the BEST order in which to put the sentences so as to form a well-organized paragraph. Each sentence has a place in the paragraph; there are no extra sentences. You are then to answer Questions 3 through 5 inclusive on the basis of your rearrangements of these scrambled sentences into a properly organized paragraph.

In 1887 some insurance companies organized an Inspection Department to advise their clients on all phases of fire prevention and protection. Probably this has been due to the smaller annual fire losses in Great Britain than in the United States. It tests various fire prevention devices and appliances and determines manufacturing hazards and their safeguards. Fire research began earlier in the United States and is more advanced than in Great Britain. Later they established a laboratory specializing in electrical, mechanical, hydraulic, and chemical fields.

3. When the five sentences are arranged in proper order, the paragraph starts with the sentence which begins 3.____
   A. "In 1887..."   B. "Probably this..."   C. "It tests..."
   D. "Fire research..."   E. "Later they..."

4. In the last sentence listed above, "they" refers to 4.____
   A. the insurance companies   B. the United States and Great Britain
   C. the Inspection Department   D. clients
   E. technicians

5. When the above paragraph is properly arranged, it ends with the words 5.____
   A. "...and protection."   B. "...the United States."
   C. "...their safeguards."   D. "...in Great Britain."
   E. "...chemical fields."

KEY (CORRECT ANSWERS)

1. C
2. C
3. D
4. A
5. C

TEST 2

DIRECTIONS: In each of the questions numbered I through V, several sentences are given. For each question, choose as your answer the group of number that represents the MOST logical order of these sentences if they were arranged in paragraph form. *PRINT THE LETTER OF THE CORRECT ANSWER IN THE SPACE AT THE RIGHT.*

1.
    I. It is established when one shows that the landlord has prevented the tenant's enjoyment of his interest in the property leased.
    II. Constructive eviction is the result of a breach of the covenant of quiet enjoyment implied in all leases.
    III. In some parts of the United States, it is not complete until the tenant vacates within a reasonable time.
    IV. Generally, the acts must be of such serious and permanent character as to deny the tenant the enjoyment of his possessing rights.
    V. In this event, upon abandonment of the premises, the tenant's liability for that ceases.
    The CORRECT answer is:
    A. II, I, IV, III, V   B. V, II, III, I, IV
    C. IV, III, I, II, V   D. I, III, V, IV, II

1.____

2.
    I. The powerlessness before private and public authorities that is the typical experience of the slum tenant is reminiscent of the situation of blue-collar workers all through the nineteenth century.
    II. Similarly, in recent years, this chapter of history has been reopened by anti-poverty groups which have attempted to organize slum tenants to enable them to bargain collectively with their landlords about the conditions of their tenancies.
    III. It is familiar history that many of the worker remedied their condition by joining together and presenting their demands collectively.
    IV. Like the workers, tenants are forced by the conditions of modern life into substantial dependence on these who possess great political aid and economic power.
    V. What's more, the very fact of dependence coupled with an absence of education and self-confidence makes them hesitant and unable to stand up for what they need from those in power.
    The CORRECT answer is:
    A. V, IV, I, II, III   B. II, III, I, V, IV
    C. III, I, V, IV, II   D. I, IV, V, III, II

2.____

3.
    I. A railroad, for example, when not acting as a common carrier may contract away responsibility for its own negligence.
    II. As to a landlord, however, no decision has been found relating to the legal effect of a clause shifting the statutory duty of repair to the tenant.
    III. The courts have not passed on the validity of clauses relieving the landlord of this duty and liability.
    IV. They have, however, upheld the validity of exculpatory clauses in other types of contracts.

3.____

V. Housing regulations impose a duty upon the landlord to maintain leased premises in safe condition.
VI. As another example, a bailee may limit his liability except for gross negligence, willful acts, or fraud.

The CORRECT answer is:
- A. II, I, VI, IV, III, V
- B. I, III, IV, V, VI, II
- C. III, V, I, IV, II, VI
- D. V, III, IV, I, VI, II

4.
I. Since there are only samples in the building, retail or consumer sales are generally eschewed by mart occupants, and in some instances, rigid controls are maintained to limit entrance to the mart only to those persons engaged in retailing.
II. Since World War I, in many larger cities, there has developed a new type of property, called the mart building.
III. It can, therefore, be used by wholesalers and jobbers for the display of sample merchandise.
IV. This type of building is most frequently a multi-storied, finished interior property which is a cross between a retail arcade and a loft building.
V. This limitation enables the mart occupants to ship the orders from another location after the retailer or dealer makes his selection from the samples.

The CORRECT answer is:
- A. II, IV, III, I, V
- B. IV, III, V, I, II
- C. I, III, II, IV, V
- D. I, IV, I, III, V

5.
I. In general, staff-line friction reduces the distinctive contribution of staff personnel.
II. The conflicts, however, introduce an uncontrolled element into the managerial system.
III. On the other hand, the natural resistance of the line to staff innovations probably usefully restrains over-eager efforts to apply untested procedures on a large scale.
IV. Under such conditions, it is difficult to know when valuable ideas are being sacrificed.
V. The relatively weak position of staff, requiring accommodation to the line, tends to restrict their ability to engage in free, experimental innovation.

The CORRECT answer is:
- A. IV, II, III, I, V
- B. I, V, III, II, IV
- C. V, III, I, II, IV
- D. II, I, IV, V, III

KEY (CORRECT ANSWERS)

1. A
2. D
3. D
4. A
5. B

TEST 3

DIRECTIONS: Questions 1 through 4 consist of six sentences which can be arranged in a logical sequence. For each question, select the choice which places the numbered sentences in the MOST logical sequent. *PRINT THE LETTER OF THE CORRECT ANSWER IN THE SPACE AT THE RIGHT.*

1. I. The burden of proof as to each issue is determined before trial and remains upon the same party throughout the trial.
    II. The jury is at liberty to believe one witness' testimony as against a number of contradictory witnesses.
    III. In a civil case, the party bearing the burden of proof is required to prove his contention by a fair preponderance of the evidence.
    IV. However, it must be noted that a fair preponderance of evidence does not necessarily mean a greater number of witnesses.
    V. The burden of proof is the burden which rests upon one of the parties to an action to persuade the trier of the facts, generally the jury, that a proposition he asserts is true.
    VI. If the evidence is equally balanced, or if it leaves the jury in such doubt as to be unable to decide the controversy either way, judgment must be given against the party upon whom the burden of proof rests.
    The CORRECT answer is:
    A. III, II, V, IV, I, VI
    B. I, II, VI, V, III, IV
    C. III, IV, V, I, II, VI
    D. V, I, III, VI, IV, II

    1.____

2. I. If a parent is without assets and is unemployed, he cannot be convicted of the crime of non-support of a child.
    II. The term "sufficient ability" has been held to mean sufficient financial ability.
    III. It does not matter if his unemployment is by choice or unavoidable circumstances.
    IV. If he fails to take any steps at all, he may be liable to prosecution for endangering the welfare of a child.
    V. Under the penal law, a parent is responsible for the support of his minor child only if the parent is "of sufficient ability."
    VI. An indigent parent may meet his obligation by borrowing money or by seeking aid under the provisions of the Social Welfare Law.
    The CORRECT answer is:
    A. VI, I, V, III, II, IV
    B. I, III, V, II, IV, VI
    C. V, II, I, III, VI, IV
    D. I, VI, IV, V, II, III

    2.____

3. I. Consider, for example, the case of a rabble rouser who urges a group of twenty people to go out and break the windows of a nearby factory.
    II. Therefore, the law fills the indicated gap with the crime of inciting to riot.
    III. A person is considered guilty of inciting to riot when he urges ten or more persons to engage in tumultuous and violent conduct of a kind likely to create public alarm.
    IV. However, if he has not obtained the cooperation of at least four people, he cannot be charged with unlawful assembly.

    3.____

131

2 (#3)

    V. The charge of inciting to riot was added to the law to cover types of conduct which cannot be classified as either the crime of "riot" or the crime of "unlawful assembly."
    VI. If he acquires the acquiescence of at least four of them, he is guilty of unlawful assembly even if the project does not materialize.
    The CORRECT answer is:
       A. III, V, I, VI, IV, II   B. V, I, IV, VI, II, III
       C. III, IV, I, V, II, VI   D. V, I, IV, VI, III, II

4.   I. If, however, the rebuttal evidence presents an issue of credibility, it is for the jury to determine whether the presumption has, in fact, been destroyed.
    II. Once sufficient evidence to the contrary is introduced, the presumption disappears from the trial.
    III. The effect of a presumption is to place the burden upon the adversary to come forward with evidence to rebut the presumption.
    IV. When a presumption is overcome and ceases to exist in the case, the fact or facts which gave rise to the presumption still remain.
    V. Whether a presumption has been overcome is ordinarily a question for the court.
    VI. Such information may furnish a basis for a logical inference.
    The CORRECT answer is:
       A. IV, VI, II, V, I, III   B. III, II, V, I, IV, VI
       C. V, III, VI, IV, II, I   D. V, IV, I, II, VI, III

4._____

KEY (CORRECT ANSWERS)

    1. D
    2. C
    3. A
    4. B

PREPARING WRITTEN MATERIAL
EXAMINATION SECTION
TEST 1

DIRECTIONS: Each question consists of a sentence which may or may not be an example of good English usage. Examine each sentence, considering grammar, punctuation, spelling, capitalization, and awkwardness. Then choose the correct statement about it from the four choices below it. If the English usage in the sentence given is better than any of the changes suggested in choices B, C, or D, pick choice A. (Do not pick a choice that will change the meaning of the sentence.) *PRINT THE LETTER OF THE CORRECT ANSWER IN THE SPACE AT THE RIGHT.*

1. We attended a staff conference on Wednesday the new safety and fire rules were discussed.
    A. This is an example of acceptable writing.
    B. The words "safety," "fire," and "rules" should begin with capital letters.
    C. There should be a comma after the word "Wednesday."
    D. There should be a period after the word "Wednesday" and the word "the" should begin with a capital letter.

1._____

2. Neither the dictionary or the telephone directory could be found in the office library.
    A. This is an example of acceptable writing.
    B. The word "or" should be changed to "nor."
    C. The word "library" should be spelled "libery."
    D. The word "neither" should be changed to "either."

2._____

3. The report would have been typed correctly if the typist could read the draft.
    A. This is an example of acceptable writing.
    B. The word "would" should be removed.
    C. The word "have" should be inserted after the word "could."
    D. The word "correctly" should be changed to "correct."

3._____

4. The supervisor brought the reports and forms to an employees desk.
    A. This is an example of acceptable writing.
    B. The word "brought" should be changed to "took."
    C. There should be a comma after the word "reports" and a comma after the word "forms."
    D. The word "employees" should be spelled "employee's."

4._____

5. It's important for all the office personnel to submit their vacation schedules on time.
    A. This is an example of acceptable writing.
    B. The word "It's" should be spelled "Its."
    C. The word "their" should be spelled "they're."
    D. The word "personnel" should be spelled "personal."

5._____

6. The report, along with the accompanying documents, were submitted for review.
    A. This is an example of acceptable writing.
    B. The words "were submitted" should be changed to "was submitted."
    C. The word "accompanying" should be spelled "accompaning."
    D. The comma after the word "report" should be taken out.

7. If others must use your files, be certain that they understand how the system works, but insist that you do all the filing and refiling.
    A. This is an example of acceptable writing.
    B. There should be a period after the word "works," and the word "but" should start a new sentence.
    C. The words "filing" and "refiling" should be spelled "fileing" and "refileing."
    D. There should be a comma after the word "but."

8. The appeal was not considered because of its late arrival.
    A. This is an example of acceptable writing.
    B. The word "its" should be changed to "it's."
    C. The word "its" should be changed to "the."
    D. The words "late arrival" should be changed to "arrival late."

9. The letter must be read carefully to determine under which subject it should be filed.
    A. This is an example of acceptable writing.
    B. The word "under" should be changed to "at."
    C. The word "determine" should be spelled "determin."
    D. The word "carefuly" should be spelled "carefully."

10. He showed potential as an office manager, but he lacked skill in delegating work.
    A. This is an example of acceptable writing.
    B. The word "delegating" should be spelled "delagating."
    C. The word "potential" should be spelled "potencial."
    D. The words "he lacked" should be changed to "was lacking."

KEY (CORRECT ANSWERS)

1.	D	6.	B
2.	B	7.	A
3.	C	8.	A
4.	D	9.	D
5.	A	10.	A

TEST 2

DIRECTIONS: Each question consists of a sentence which may or may not be an example of good English usage. Examine each sentence, considering grammar, punctuation, spelling, capitalization, and awkwardness. Then choose the correct statement about it from the four choices below it. If the English usage in the sentence given is better than any of the changes suggested in choices B, C, or D, pick choice A. (Do not pick a choice that will change the meaning of the sentence.) *PRINT THE LETTER OF THE CORRECT ANSWER IN THE SPACE AT THE RIGHT.*

1. The supervisor wants that all staff members report to the office at 9:00 A.M.   1._____
   A. This is an example of acceptable writing.
   B. The word "that" should be removed and the word "to" should be inserted after the word "members."
   C. There should be a comma after the word "wants" and a comma after the word "office."
   D. The word "wants" should be changed to "want" and the word "shall" should be inserted after the word "members."

2. Every morning the clerk opens the office mail and distributes it.   2._____
   A. This is an example of acceptable writing.
   B. The word "opens" should be changed to "open."
   C. The word "mail" should be changed to "letters."
   D. The word "it" should be changed to "them."

3. The secretary typed more fast on a desktop computer than on a laptop computer.   3._____
   A. This is an example of acceptable writing.
   B. The words "more fast" should be changed to "faster."
   C. There should be a comma after the words "desktop computer."
   D. The word "than" should be changed to "then."

4. The new stenographer needed a desk a computer, a chair and a blotter.   4._____
   A. This is an example of acceptable writing.
   B. The word "blotter" should be spelled "blodder."
   C. The word "stenographer" should begin with a capital letter.
   D. There should be a comma after the word "desk."

5. The recruiting officer said, "There are many different goverment jobs available."   5._____
   A. This is an example of acceptable writing.
   B. The word "There" should not be capitalized.
   C. The word "government" should be spelled "government."
   D. The comma after the word "said" should be removed.

6. He can recommend a mechanic whose work is reliable.   6._____
   A. This is an example of acceptable writing.
   B. The word "reliable" should be spelled "relyable."
   C. The word "whose" should be spelled "who's."
   D. The word "mechanic should be spelled "mecanic."

7. She typed quickly; like someone who had not a moment to lose. 7.____
   A. This is an example of acceptable writing.
   B. The word "not" should be removed.
   C. The semicolon should be changed to a comma.
   D. The word "quickly" should be placed before instead of after the word "typed."

8. She insisted that she had to much work to do. 8.____
   A. This is an example of acceptable writing.
   B. The word "insisted" should be spelled "incisted."
   C. The word "to" used in front of "much" should be spelled "too."
   D. The word "do" should be changed to "be done."

9. He excepted praise from his supervisor for a job well done. 9.____
   A. This is an example of acceptable writing.
   B. The word "excepted" should be spelled "accepted."
   C. The order of the words "well done" should be changed to "done well."
   D. There should be a comma after the word "supervisor."

10. What appears to be intentional errors in grammar occur several times in the passage. 10.____
    A. This is an example of acceptable writing.
    B. The word "occur" should be spelled "occurr."
    C. The word "appears" should be changed to "appear."
    D. The phrase "several times" should be changed to "from time to time."

KEY (CORRECT ANSWERS)

1. B
2. A
3. B
4. D
5. C
6. A
7. C
8. C
9. B
10. C

TEST 3

DIRECTIONS: Each question consists of a sentence which may or may not be an example of good English usage. Examine each sentence, considering grammar, punctuation, spelling, capitalization, and awkwardness. Then choose the correct statement about it from the four choices below it. If the English usage in the sentence given is better than any of the changes suggested in choices B, C, or D, pick choice A. (Do not pick a choice that will change the meaning of the sentence.) *PRINT THE LETTER OF THE CORRECT ANSWER IN THE SPACE AT THE RIGHT.*

1. The clerk could have completed the assignment on time if he knows where these materials were located.
    A. This is an example of acceptable writing.
    B. The word "knows" should be replaced by "had known."
    C. The word "were" should be replaced by "had been."
    D. The words "where these materials were located" should be replaced by "the location of these materials."

    1.____

2. All employees should be given safety training. Not just those who accidents.
    A. This is an example of acceptable writing.
    B. The period after the word "training" should be changed to a colon.
    C. The period after the word "training" should be changed to a semicolon, and the first letter of the word "Not" should be changed to a small "n."
    D. The period after the word "training" should be changed to a comma, and the first letter of the word "Not" should be changed to a small "n."

    2.____

3. This proposal is designed to promote employee awareness of the suggestion program, to encourage employee participation in the program, and to increase the number of suggestions submitted.
    A. This is an example of acceptable writing.
    B. The word "proposal" should be spelled "proposal."
    C. The words "to increase the number of suggestions submitted" should be changed to "an increase in the number of suggestions is expected."
    D. The word "promote" should be changed to "enhance" and the word "increase" should be changed to "add to."

    3.____

4. The introduction of inovative managerial techniques should be preceded by careful analysis of the specific circumstances and conditions in each department.
    A. This is an example of acceptable writing.
    B. The word "technique" should be spelled "techneques."
    C. The word "inovative" should be spelled "innovative."
    D. A comma should be placed after the word "circumstances" and after the word "conditions."

    4.____

5. This occurrence indicates that such criticism embarrasses him.
    A. This is an example of acceptable writing.
    B. The word "occurrence" should be spelled "occurence."
    C. The word "criticism" should be spelled "critisism."
    D. The word "embarrasses" should be spelled "embarasses."

5._____

KEY (CORRECT ANSWERS)

1. B
2. D
3. A
4. C
5. A

PHILOSOPHY, PRINCIPLES, PRACTICES AND TECHNICS OF SUPERVISION, ADMINISTRATION, MANAGEMENT AND ORGANIZATION

TABLE OF CONTENTS

		Page
I.	MEANING OF SUPERVISION	1
II.	THE OLD AND THE NEW SUPERVISION	1
III.	THE EIGHT (8) BASIC PRINCIPLES OF THE NEW SUPERVISION	1
	1. Principle of Responsibility	1
	2. Principle of Authority	2
	3. Principle of Self-Growth	2
	4. Principle of Individual Worth	2
	5. Principle of Creative Leadership	2
	6. Principle of Success and Failure	2
	7. Principle of Science	3
	8. Principle of Cooperation	3
IV.	WHAT IS ADMINISTRATION?	3
	1. Practices commonly classed as "Supervisory"	3
	2. Practices commonly classed as "Administrative"	3
	3. Practices classified as both "Supervisory" and "Administrative"	4
V.	RESPONSIBILITIES OF THE SUPERVISOR	4
VI.	COMPETENCIES OF THE SUPERVISOR	4
VII.	THE PROFESSIONAL SUPERVISOR—EMPLOYEE RELATIONSHIP	4
VIII.	MINI-TEXT IN SUPERVISION, ADMINISTRATION, MANAGEMENT AND ORGANIZATION	5
	A. Brief Highlights	5
	1. Levels of Management	5
	2. What the Supervisor Must Learn	6
	3. A Definition of Supervision	6
	4. Elements of the Team Concept	6
	5. Principles of Organization	6
	6. The Four Important Parts of Every Job	6
	7. Principles of Delegation	6
	8. Principles of Effective Communications	7
	9. Principles of Work Improvement	7

TABLE OF CONTENTS (CONTINUED)

  10. Areas of Job Improvement   7
  11. Seven Key Points in Making Improvements   7
  12. Corrective Techniques for Job Improvement   7
  13. A Planning Checklist   8
  14. Five Characteristics of Good Directions   8
  15. Types of Directions   8
  16. Controls   8
  17. Orienting the New Employee   8
  18. Checklist for Orienting New Employees   8
  19. Principles of Learning   9
  20. Causes of Poor Performance   9
  21. Four Major Steps in On-The-Job Instructions   9
  22. Employees Want Five Things   9
  23. Some Don'ts in Regard to Praise   9
  24. How to Gain Your Workers' Confidence   9
  25. Sources of Employee Problems   9
  26. The Supervisor's Key to Discipline   10
  27. Five Important Processes of Management   10
  28. When the Supervisor Fails to Plan   10
  29. Fourteen General Principles of Management   10
  30. Change   10

 B. Brief Topical Summaries   11
  I. Who/What is the Supervisor?   11
  II. The Sociology of Work   11
  III. Principles and Practices of Supervision   12
  IV. Dynamic Leadership   12
  V. Processes for Solving Problems   12
  VI. Training for Results   13
  VII. Health, Safety and Accident Prevention   13
  VIII. Equal Employment Opportunity   13
  IX. Improving Communications   14
  X. Self-Development   14
  XI. Teaching and Training   14
   A. The Teaching Process   14
    1. Preparation   14
    2. Presentation   15
    3. Summary   15
    4. Application   15
    5. Evaluation   15
   B. Teaching Methods   15
    1. Lecture   15
    2. Discussion   15
    3. Demonstration   16
    4. Performance   16
    5. Which Method to Use   16

PHILOSOPHY, PRINCIPLES, PRACTICES, AND TECHNICS
OF
SUPERVISION, ADMINISTRATION, MANAGEMENT AND ORGANIZATION

I. MEANING OF SUPERVISION

The extension of the democratic philosophy has been accompanied by an extension in the scope of supervision. Modern leaders and supervisors no longer think of supervision in the narrow sense of being confined chiefly to visiting employees, supplying materials, or rating the staff. They regard supervision as being intimately related to all the concerned agencies of society, they speak of the supervisor's function in terms of "growth", rather than the "improvement," of employees.

This modern concept of supervision may be defined as follows:

Supervision is leadership and the development of leadership within groups which are cooperatively engaged in inspection, research, training, guidance and evaluation.

II. THE OLD AND THE NEW SUPERVISION

TRADITIONAL
1. Inspection
2. Focused on the employee
3. Visitation
4. Random and haphazard
5. Imposed and authoritarian
6. One person usually

MODERN
1. Study and analysis
2. Focused on aims, materials, methods, supervisors, employees, environment
3. Demonstrations, intervisitation, workshops, directed reading, bulletins, etc.
4. Definitely organized and planned (scientific)
5. Cooperative and democratic
6. Many persons involved (creative)

III THE EIGHT (8) BASIC PRINCIPLES OF THE NEW SUPERVISION

1. *PRINCIPLE OF RESPONSIBILITY*
Authority to act and responsibility for acting must be joined.
   a. If you give responsibility, give authority.
   b. Define employee duties clearly.
   c. Protect employees from criticism by others.
   d. Recognize the rights as well as obligations of employees.
   e. Achieve the aims of a democratic society insofar as it is possible within the area of your work.
   f. Establish a situation favorable to training and learning.
   g. Accept ultimate responsibility for everything done in your section, unit, office, division, department.
   h. Good administration and good supervision are inseparable.

2. PRINCIPLE OF AUTHORITY

The success of the supervisor is measured by the extent to which the power of authority is not used.

    a. Exercise simplicity and informality in supervision.
    b. Use the simplest machinery of supervision.
    c. If it is good for the organization as a whole, it is probably justified.
    d. Seldom be arbitrary or authoritative.
    e. Do not base your work on the power of position or of personality.
    f. Permit and encourage the free expression of opinions.

3. PRINCIPLE OF SELF-GROWTH

The success of the supervisor is measured by the extent to which, and the speed with which, he is no longer needed.

    a. Base criticism on principles, not on specifics.
    b. Point out higher activities to employees.
    c. Train for self-thinking by employees, to meet new situations.
    d. Stimulate initiative, self-reliance and individual responsibility.
    e. Concentrate on stimulating the growth of employees rather than on removing defects.

4. PRINCIPLE OF INDIVIDUAL WORTH

Respect for the individual is a paramount consideration in supervision.

    a. Be human and sympathetic in dealing with employees.
    b. Don't nag about things to be done.
    c. Recognize the individual differences among employees and seek opportunities to permit best expression of each personality.

5. PRINCIPLE OF CREATIVE LEADERSHIP

The best supervision is that which is not apparent to the employee.

    a. Stimulate, don't drive employees to creative action.
    b. Emphasize doing good things.
    c. Encourage employees to do what they do best.
    d. Do not be too greatly concerned with details of subject or method.
    e. Do not be concerned exclusively with immediate problems and activities.
    f. Reveal higher activities and make them both desired and maximally possible.
    g. Determine procedures in the light of each situation but see that these are derived from a sound basic philosophy.
    h. Aid, inspire and lead so as to liberate the creative spirit latent in all good employees.

6. PRINCIPLE OF SUCCESS AND FAILURE

There are no unsuccessful employees, only unsuccessful supervisors who have failed to give proper leadership.

    a. Adapt suggestions to the capacities, attitudes, and prejudices of employees.
    b. Be gradual, be progressive, be persistent.
    c. Help the employee find the general principle; have the employee apply his own problem to the general principle.
    d. Give adequate appreciation for good work and honest effort.
    e. Anticipate employee difficulties and help to prevent them.
    f. Encourage employees to do the desirable things they will do anyway.
    g. Judge your supervision by the results it secures.

7. PRINCIPLE OF SCIENCE

Successful supervision is scientific, objective, and experimental. It is based on facts, not on prejudices.

    a. Be cumulative in results.
    b. Never divorce your suggestions from the goals of training.
    c. Don't be impatient of results.
    d. Keep all matters on a professional, not a personal level.
    e. Do not be concerned exclusively with immediate problems and activities.
    f. Use objective means of determining achievement and rating where possible.

8. PRINCIPLE OF COOPERATION

Supervision is a cooperative enterprise between supervisor and employee.

    a. Begin with conditions as they are.
    b. Ask opinions of all involved when formulating policies.
    c. Organization is as good as its weakest link.
    d. Let employees help to determine policies and department programs.
    e. Be approachable and accessible - physically and mentally.
    f. Develop pleasant social relationships.

IV. WHAT IS ADMINISTRATION?

Administration is concerned with providing the environment, the material facilities, and the operational procedures that will promote the maximum growth and development of supervisors and employees. (Organization is an aspect, and a concomitant, of administration.)

There is no sharp line of demarcation between supervision and administration; these functions are intimately interrelated and, often, overlapping. They are complementary activities.

1. PRACTICES COMMONLY CLASSED AS "SUPERVISORY"

    a. Conducting employees conferences
    b. Visiting sections, units, offices, divisions, departments
    c. Arranging for demonstrations
    d. Examining plans
    e. Suggesting professional reading
    f. Interpreting bulletins
    g. Recommending in-service training courses
    h. Encouraging experimentation
    i. Appraising employee morale
    j. Providing for intervisitation

2. PRACTICES COMMONLY CLASSIFIED AS "ADMINISTRATIVE"

    a. Management of the office
    b. Arrangement of schedules for extra duties
    c. Assignment of rooms or areas
    d. Distribution of supplies
    e. Keeping records and reports
    f. Care of audio-visual materials
    g. Keeping inventory records
    h. Checking record cards and books
    i. Programming special activities
    j. Checking on the attendance and punctuality of employees

3. *PRACTICES COMMONLY CLASSIFIED AS BOTH "SUPERVISORY" AND "ADMINISTRATIVE"*
   a. Program construction
   b. Testing or evaluating outcomes
   c. Personnel accounting
   d. Ordering instructional materials

V. RESPONSIBILITIES OF THE SUPERVISOR

A person employed in a supervisory capacity must constantly be able to improve his own efficiency and ability. He represents the employer to the employees and only continuous self-examination can make him a capable supervisor.

Leadership and training are the supervisor's responsibility. An efficient working unit is one in which the employees work with the supervisor. It is his job to bring out the best in his employees. He must always be relaxed, courteous and calm in his association with his employees. Their feelings are important, and a harsh attitude does not develop the most efficient employees.

VI. COMPETENCIES OF THE SUPERVISOR

1. Complete knowledge of the duties and responsibilities of his position.
2. To be able to organize a job, plan ahead and carry through.
3. To have self-confidence and initiative.
4. To be able to handle the unexpected situation and make quick decisions.
5. To be able to properly train subordinates in the positions they are best suited for.
6. To be able to keep good human relations among his subordinates.
7. To be able to keep good human relations between his subordinates and himself and to earn their respect and trust.

VII. THE PROFESSIONAL SUPERVISOR-EMPLOYEE RELATIONSHIP

There are two kinds of efficiency: one kind is only apparent and is produced in organizations through the exercise of mere discipline; this is but a simulation of the second, or true, efficiency which springs from spontaneous cooperation. If you are a manager, no matter how great or small your responsibility, it is your job, in the final analysis, to create and develop this involuntary cooperation among the people whom you supervise. For, no matter how powerful a combination of money, machines, and materials a company may have, this is a dead and sterile thing without a team of willing, thinking and articulate people to guide it.

The following 21 points are presented as indicative of the exemplary basic relationship that should exist between supervisor and employee:

1. Each person wants to be liked and respected by his fellow employee and wants to be treated with consideration and respect by his superior.
2. The most competent employee will make an error. However, in a unit where good relations exist between the supervisor and his employees, tenseness and fear do not exist. Thus, errors are not hidden or covered up and the efficiency of a unit is not impaired.
3. Subordinates resent rules, regulations, or orders that are unreasonable or unexplained.
4. Subordinates are quick to resent unfairness, harshness, injustices and favoritism.
5. An employee will accept responsibility if he knows that he will be complimented for a job well done, and not too harshly chastised for failure; that his supervisor will check the cause of the failure, and, if it was the supervisor's fault, he will assume the blame therefore. If it was the employee's fault, his supervisor will explain the correct method or means of handling the responsibility.

6. An employee wants to receive credit for a suggestion he has made, that is used. If a suggestion cannot be used, the employee is entitled to an explanation. The supervisor should not say "no" and close the subject.
7. Fear and worry slow up a worker's ability. Poor working environment can impair his physical and mental health. A good supervisor avoids forceful methods, threats and arguments to get a job done.
8. A forceful supervisor is able to train his employees individually and as a team, and is able to motivate them in the proper channels.
9. A mature supervisor is able to properly evaluate his subordinates and to keep them happy and satisfied.
10. A sensitive supervisor will never patronize his subordinates.
11. A worthy supervisor will respect his employees' confidences.
12. Definite and clear-cut responsibilities should be assigned to each executive.
13. Responsibility should always be coupled with corresponding authority.
14. No change should be made in the scope or responsibilities of a position without a definite understanding to that effect on the part of all persons concerned.
15. No executive or employee, occupying a single position in the organization, should be subject to definite orders from more than one source.
16. Orders should never be given to subordinates over the head of a responsible executive. Rather than do this, the officer in question should be supplanted.
17. Criticisms of subordinates should, whoever possible, be made privately, and in no case should a subordinate be criticized in the presence of executives or employees of equal or lower rank.
18. No dispute or difference between executives or employees as to authority or responsibilities should be considered too trivial for prompt and careful adjudication.
19. Promotions, wage changes, and disciplinary action should always be approved by the executive immediately superior to the one directly responsible.
20. No executive or employee should ever be required, or expected, to be at the same time an assistant to, and critic of, another.
21. Any executive whose work is subject to regular inspection should, whever practicable, be given the assistance and facilities necessary to enable him to maintain an independent check of the quality of his work.

VIII. MINI-TEXT IN SUPERVISION, ADMINISTRATION, MANAGEMENT, AND ORGANIZATION

A. BRIEF HIGHLIGHTS

Listed concisely and sequentially are major headings and important data in the field for quick recall and review.

1. *LEVELS OF MANAGEMENT*

Any organization of some size has several levels of management. In terms of a ladder the levels are:

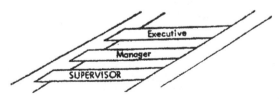

The first level is very important because it is the beginning point of management leadership.

2. WHAT THE SUPERVISOR MUST LEARN
A supervisor must learn to:
- (1) Deal with people and their differences
- (2) Get the job done through people
- (3) Recognize the problems when they exist
- (4) Overcome obstacles to good performance
- (5) Evaluate the performance of people
- (6) Check his own performance in terms of accomplishment

3. A DEFINITION OF SUPERVISOR
The term supervisor means any individual having authority, in the interests of the employer, to hire, transfer, suspend, lay-off, recall, promote, discharge, assign, reward, or discipline other employees or responsibility to direct them, or to adjust their grievances, or effectively to recommend such action, if, in connection with the foregoing, exercise of such authority is not of a merely routine or clerical nature but requires the use of independent judgment.

4. ELEMENTS OF THE TEAM CONCEPT
What is involved in teamwork? The component parts are:
- (1) Members
- (2) A leader
- (3) Goals
- (4) Plans
- (5) Cooperation
- (6) Spirit

5. PRINCIPLES OF ORGANIZATION
- (1) A team member must know what his job is.
- (2) Be sure that the nature and scope of a job are understood.
- (3) Authority and responsibility should be carefully spelled out.
- (4) A supervisor should be permitted to make the maximum number of decisions affecting his employees.
- (5) Employees should report to only one supervisor.
- (6) A supervisor should direct only as many employees as he can handle effectively.
- (7) An organization plan should be flexible.
- (8) Inspection and performance of work should be separate.
- (9) Organizational problems should receive immediate attention.
- (10) Assign work in line with ability and experience.

6. THE FOUR IMPORTANT PARTS OF EVERY JOB
- (1) Inherent in every job is the *accountability* for results.
- (2) A second set of factors in every job is *responsibilities.*
- (3) Along with duties and responsibilities one must have the *authority* to act within certain limits without obtaining permission to proceed.
- (4) No job exists in a vacuum. The supervisor is surrounded by key *relationships.*

7. PRINCIPLES OF DELEGATION
Where work is delegated for the first time, the supervisor should think in terms of these questions:
- (1) Who is best qualified to do this?
- (2) Can an employee improve his abilities by doing this?
- (3) How long should an employee spend on this?
- (4) Are there any special problems for which he will need guidance?
- (5) How broad a delegation can I make?

8. PRINCIPLES OF EFFECTIVE COMMUNICATIONS
  (1) Determine the media
  (2) To whom directed?
  (3) Identification and source authority
  (4) Is communication understood?

9. PRINCIPLES OF WORK IMPROVEMENT
  (1) Most people usually do only the work which is assigned to them
  (2) Workers are likely to fit assigned work into the time available to perform it
  (3) A good workload usually stimulates output
  (4) People usually do their best work when they know that results will be reviewed or inspected
  (5) Employees usually feel that someone else is responsible for conditions of work, workplace layout, job methods, type of tools/equipment, and other such factors
  (6) Employees are usually defensive about their job security
  (7) Employees have natural resistance to change
  (8) Employees can support or destroy a supervisor
  (9) A supervisor usually earns the respect of his people through his personal example of diligence and efficiency

10. AREAS OF JOB IMPROVEMENT
The areas of job improvement are quite numerous, but the most common ones which a supervisor can identify and utilize are:
  (1) Departmental layout
  (2) Flow of work
  (3) Workplace layout
  (4) Utilization of manpower
  (5) Work methods
  (6) Materials handling
  (7) Utilization
  (8) Motion economy

11. SEVEN KEY POINTS IN MAKING IMPROVEMENTS
  (1) Select the job to be improved
  (2) Study how it is being done now
  (3) Question the present method
  (4) Determine actions to be taken
  (5) Chart proposed method
  (6) Get approval and apply
  (7) Solicit worker participation

12. CORRECTIVE TECHNIQUES OF JOB IMPROVEMENT

Specific Problems	General Improvement	Corrective Techniques
(1) Size of workload	(1) Departmental layout	(1) Study with scale model
(2) Inability to meet schedules	(2) Flow of work	(2) Flow chart study
(3) Strain and fatigue	(3) Work plan layout	(3) Motion analysis
(4) Improper use of men and skills	(4) Utilization of manpower	(4) Comparison of units produced to standard allowance
(5) Waste, poor quality, unsafe conditions	(5) Work methods	(5) Methods analysis
(6) Bottleneck conditions that hinder output	(6) Materials handling	(6) Flow chart & equipment study
(7) Poor utilization of equipment and machine	(7) Utilization of equipment	(7) Down time vs. running time
(8) Efficiency and productivity of labor	(8) Motion economy	(8) Motion analysis

13. *A PLANNING CHECKLIST*
   - (1) Objectives
   - (2) Controls
   - (3) Delegations
   - (4) Communications
   - (5) Resources
   - (6) Resources
   - (7) Manpower
   - (8) Equipment
   - (9) Supplies and materials
   - (10) Utilization of time
   - (11) Safety
   - (12) Money
   - (13) Work
   - (14) Timing of improvements

14. *FIVE CHARACTERISTICS OF GOOD DIRECTIONS*
   In order to get results, directions must be:
   - (1) Possible of accomplishment
   - (2) Agreeable with worker interests
   - (3) Related to mission
   - (4) Planned and complete
   - (5) Unmistakably clear

15. *TYPES OF DIRECTIONS*
   - (1) Demands or direct orders
   - (2) Requests
   - (3) Suggestion or implication
   - (4) Volunteering

16. *CONTROLS*
   A typical listing of the overall areas in which the supervisor should establish controls might be:
   - (1) Manpower
   - (2) Materials
   - (3) Quality of work
   - (4) Quantity of work
   - (5) Time
   - (6) Space
   - (7) Money
   - (8) Methods

17. *ORIENTING THE NEW EMPLOYEE*
   - (1) Prepare for him
   - (2) Welcome the new employee
   - (3) Orientation for the job
   - (4) Follow-up

18. *CHECKLIST FOR ORIENTING NEW EMPLOYEES*   Yes   No
   - (1) Do your appreciate the feelings of new employees when they first report for work?
   - (2) Are you aware of the fact that the new employee must make a big adjustment to his job?
   - (3) Have you given him good reasons for liking the job and the organization?
   - (4) Have you prepared for his first day on the job?
   - (5) Did you welcome him cordially and make him feel needed?
   - (6) Did you establish rapport with him so that he feels free to talk and discuss matters with you?
   - (7) Did you explain his job to him and his relationship to you?
   - (8) Does he know that his work will be evaluated periodically on a basis that is fair and objective?
   - (9) Did you introduce him to his fellow workers in such a way that they are likely to accept him?
   - (10) Does he know what employee benefits he will receive?
   - (11) Does he understand the importance of being on the job and what to do if he must leave his duty station?
   - (12) Has he been impressed with the importance of accident prevention and safe practice?
   - (13) Does he generally know his way around the department?
   - (14) Is he under the guidance of a sponsor who will teach the right ways of doing things?
   - (15) Do you plan to follow-up so that he will continue to adjust successfully to his job?

19. *PRINCIPLES OF LEARNING*
    (1) Motivation   (2) Demonstration or explanation   (3) Practice

20. *CAUSES OF POOR PERFORMANCE*
    (1) Improper training for job
    (2) Wrong tools
    (3) Inadequate directions
    (4) Lack of supervisory follow-up
    (5) Poor communications
    (6) Lack of standards of performance
    (7) Wrong work habits
    (8) Low morale
    (9) Other

21. *FOUR MAJOR STEPS IN ON-THE-JOB INSTRUCTION*
    (1) Prepare the worker
    (2) Present the operation
    (3) Tryout performance
    (4) Follow-up

22. *EMPLOYEES WANT FIVE THINGS*
    (1) Security   (2) Opportunity   (3) Recognition   (4) Inclusion   (5) Expression

23. *SOME DON'TS IN REGARD TO PRAISE*
    (1) Don't praise a person for something he hasn't done
    (2) Don't praise a person unless you can be sincere
    (3) Don't be sparing in praise just because your superior withholds it from you
    (4) Don't let too much time elapse between good performance and recognition of it

24. *HOW TO GAIN YOUR WORKERS' CONFIDENCE*
    Methods of developing confidence include such things as:
    (1) Knowing the interests, habits, hobbies of employees
    (2) Admitting your own inadequacies
    (3) Sharing and telling of confidence in others
    (4) Supporting people when they are in trouble
    (5) Delegating matters that can be well handled
    (6) Being frank and straightforward about problems and working conditions
    (7) Encouraging others to bring their problems to you
    (8) Taking action on problems which impede worker progress

25. *SOURCES OF EMPLOYEE PROBLEMS*
    On-the-job causes might be such things as:
    (1) A feeling that favoritism is exercised in assignments
    (2) Assignment of overtime
    (3) An undue amount of supervision
    (4) Changing methods or systems
    (5) Stealing of ideas or trade secrets
    (6) Lack of interest in job
    (7) Threat of reduction in force
    (8) Ignorance or lack of communications
    (9) Poor equipment
    (10) Lack of knowing how supervisor feels toward employee
    (11) Shift assignments

    Off-the-job problems might have to do with:
    (1) Health   (2) Finances   (3) Housing   (4) Family

26. THE SUPERVISOR'S KEY TO DISCIPLINE

There are several key points about discipline which the supervisor should keep in mind:
(1) Job discipline is one of the disciplines of life and is directed by the supervisor.
(2) It is more important to correct an employee fault than to fix blame for it.
(3) Employee performance is affected by problems both on the job and off.
(4) Sudden or abrupt changes in behavior can be indications of important employee problems.
(5) Problems should be dealt with as soon as possible after they are identified.
(6) The attitude of the supervisor may have more to do with solving problems than the techniques of problem solving.
(7) Correction of employee behavior should be resorted to only after the supervisor is sure that training or counseling will not be helpful.
(8) Be sure to document your disciplinary actions.
(9) Make sure that you are disciplining on the basis of facts rather than personal feelings.
(10) Take each disciplinary step in order, being careful not to make snap judgments, or decisions based on impatience.

27. FIVE IMPORTANT PROCESSES OF MANAGEMENT

(1) Planning (2) Organizing (3) Scheduling
(4) Controlling (5) Motivating

28. WHEN THE SUPERVISOR FAILS TO PLAN

(1) Supervisor creates impression of not knowing his job
(2) May lead to excessive overtime
(3) Job runs itself -- supervisor lacks control
(4) Deadlines and appointments missed
(5) Parts of the work go undone
(6) Work interrupted by emergencies
(7) Sets a bad example
(8) Uneven workload creates peaks and valleys
(9) Too much time on minor details at expense of more important tasks

29. FOURTEEN GENERAL PRINCIPLES OF MANAGEMENT

(1) Division of work
(2) Authority and responsibility
(3) Discipline
(4) Unity of command
(5) Unity of direction
(6) Subordination of individual interest to general interest
(7) Remuneration of personnel
(8) Centralization
(9) Scalar chain
(10) Order
(11) Equity
(12) Stability of tenure of personnel
(13) Initiative
(14) Esprit de corps

30. CHANGE

Bringing about change is perhaps attempted more often, and yet less well understood, than anything else the supervisor does. How do people generally react to change? (People tend to resist change that is imposed upon them by other individuals or circumstances.

Change is characteristic of every situation. It is a part of every real endeavor where the efforts of people are concerned.

A. Why do people resist change?
   People may resist change because of:
   (1) Fear of the unknown
   (2) Implied criticism
   (3) Unpleasant experiences in the past
   (4) Fear of loss of status
   (5) Threat to the ego
   (6) Fear of loss of economic stability

B. How can we best overcome the resistance to change?
   In initiating change, take these steps:
   (1) Get ready to sell
   (2) Identify sources of help
   (3) Anticipate objections
   (4) Sell benefits
   (5) Listen in depth
   (6) Follow up

B. BRIEF TOPICAL SUMMARIES

I. WHO/WHAT IS THE SUPERVISOR?
1. The supervisor is often called the "highest level employee and the lowest level manager."
2. A supervisor is a member of both management and the work group. He acts as a bridge between the two.
3. Most problems in supervision are in the area of human relations, or people problems.
4. Employees expect: Respect, opportunity to learn and to advance, and a sense of belonging, and so forth.
5. Supervisors are responsible for directing people and organizing work. Planning is of paramount importance.
6. A position description is a set of duties and responsibilities inherent to a given position.
7. It is important to keep the position description up-to-date and to provide each employee with his own copy.

II. THE SOCIOLOGY OF WORK
1. People are alike in many ways; however, each individual is unique.
2. The supervisor is challenged in getting to know employee differences. Acquiring skills in evaluating individuals is an asset.
3. Maintaining meaningful working relationships in the organization is of great importance.
4. The supervisor has an obligation to help individuals to develop to their fullest potential.
5. Job rotation on a planned basis helps to build versatility and to maintain interest and enthusiasm in work groups.
6. Cross training (job rotation) provides backup skills.
7. The supervisor can help reduce tension by maintaining a sense of humor, providing guidance to employees, and by making reasonable and timely decisions. Employees respond favorably to working under reasonably predictable circumstances.
8. Change is characteristic of all managerial behavior. The supervisor must adjust to changes in procedures, new methods, technological changes, and to a number of new and sometimes challenging situations.
9. To overcome the natural tendency for people to resist change, the supervisor should become more skillful in initiating change.

III. PRINCIPLES AND PRACTICES OF SUPERVISION

1. Employees should be required to answer to only one superior.
2. A supervisor can effectively direct only a limited number of employees, depending upon the complexity, variety, and proximity of the jobs involved.
3. The organizational chart presents the organization in graphic form. It reflects lines of authority and responsibility as well as interrelationships of units within the organization.
4. Distribution of work can be improved through an analysis using the "Work Distribution Chart."
5. The "Work Distribution Chart" reflects the division of work within a unit in understandable form.
6. When related tasks are given to an employee, he has a better chance of increasing his skills through training.
7. The individual who is given the responsibility for tasks must also be given the appropriate authority to insure adequate results.
8. The supervisor should delegate repetitive, routine work. Preparation of recurring reports, maintaining leave and attendance records are some examples.
9. Good discipline is essential to good task performance. Discipline is reflected in the actions of employees on the job in the absence of supervision.
10. Disciplinary action may have to be taken when the positive aspects of discipline have failed. Reprimand, warning, and suspension are examples of disciplinary action.
11. If a situation calls for a reprimand, be sure it is deserved and remember it is to be done in private.

IV. DYNAMIC LEADERSHIP

1. A style is a personal method or manner of exerting influence.
2. Authoritarian leaders often see themselves as the source of power and authority.
3. The democratic leader often perceives the group as the source of authority and power.
4. Supervisors tend to do better when using the pattern of leadership that is most natural for them.
5. Social scientists suggest that the effective supervisor use the leadership style that best fits the problem or circumstances involved.
6. All four styles -- telling, selling, consulting, joining -- have their place. Using one does not preclude using the other at another time.
7. The theory X point of view assumes that the average person dislikes work, will avoid it whenever possible, and must be coerced to achieve organizational objectives.
8. The theory Y point of view assumes that the average person considers work to be as natural as play, and, when the individual is committed, he requires little supervision or direction to accomplish desired objectives.
9. The leader's basic assumptions concerning human behavior and human nature affect his actions, decisions, and other managerial practices.
10. Dissatisfaction among employees is often present, but difficult to isolate. The supervisor should seek to weaken dissatisfaction by keeping promises, being sincere and considerate, keeping employees informed, and so forth.
11. Constructive suggestions should be encouraged during the natural progress of the work.

V. PROCESSES FOR SOLVING PROBLEMS

1. People find their daily tasks more meaningful and satisfying when they can improve them.
2. The causes of problems, or the key factors, are often hidden in the background. Ability to solve problems often involves the ability to isolate them from their backgrounds. There is some substance to the cliché that some persons "can't see the forest for the trees."
3. New procedures are often developed from old ones. Problems should be broken down into manageable parts. New ideas can be adapted from old ones.

4. People think differently in problem-solving situations. Using a logical, patterned approach is often useful. One approach found to be useful includes these steps:
   - (a) Define the problem
   - (b) Establish objectives
   - (c) Get the facts
   - (d) Weigh and decide
   - (e) Take action
   - (f) Evaluate action

VI. TRAINING FOR RESULTS
1. Participants respond best when they feel training is important to them.
2. The supervisor has responsibility for the training and development of those who report to him.
3. When training is delegated to others, great care must be exercised to insure the trainer has knowledge, aptitude, and interest for his work as a trainer.
4. Training (learning) of some type goes on continually. The most successful supervisor makes certain the learning contributes in a productive manner to operational goals.
5. New employees are particularly susceptible to training. Older employees facing new job situations require specific training, as well as having need for development and growth opportunities.
6. Training needs require continuous monitoring.
7. The training officer of an agency is a professional with a responsibility to assist supervisors in solving training problems.
8. Many of the self-development steps important to the supervisor's own growth are equally important to the development of peers and subordinates. Knowledge of these is important when the supervisor consults with others on development and growth opportunities.

VII. HEALTH, SAFETY, AND ACCIDENT PREVENTION
1. Management-minded supervisors take appropriate measures to assist employees in maintaining health and in assuring safe practices in the work environment.
2. Effective safety training and practices help to avoid injury and accidents.
3. Safety should be a management goal. All infractions of safety which are observed should be corrected without exception.
4. Employees' safety attitude, training and instruction, provision of safe tools and equipment, supervision, and leadership are considered highly important factors which contribute to safety and which can be influenced directly by supervisors.
5. When accidents do occur they should be investigated promptly for very important reasons, including the fact that information which is gained can be used to prevent accidents in the future.

VIII. EQUAL EMPLOYMENT OPPORTUNITY
1. The supervisor should endeavor to treat all employees fairly, without regard to religion, race, sex, or national origin.
2. Groups tend to reflect the attitude of the leader. Prejudice can be detected even in very subtle form. Supervisors must strive to create a feeling of mutual respect and confidence in every employee.
3. Complete utilization of all human resources is a national goal. Equitable consideration should be accorded women in the work force, minority-group members, the physically and mentally handicapped, and the older employee. The important question is: "Who can do the job?"
4. Training opportunities, recognition for performance, overtime assignments, promotional opportunities, and all other personnel actions are to be handled on an equitable basis.

IX. IMPROVING COMMUNICATIONS

1. Communications is achieving understanding between the sender and the receiver of a message. It also means sharing information -- the creation of understanding.
2. Communication is basic to all human activity. Words are means of conveying meanings; however, real meanings are in people.
3. There are very practical differences in the effectiveness of one-way, impersonal, and two-way communications. Words spoken face-to-face are better understood. Telephone conversations are effective, but lack the rapport of person-to-person exchanges. The whole person communicates.
4. Cooperation and communication in an organization go hand in hand. When there is a mutual respect between people, spelling out rules and procedures for communicating is unnecessary.
5. There are several barriers to effective communications. These include failure to listen with respect and understanding, lack of skill in feedback, and misinterpreting the meanings of words used by the speaker. It is also common practice to listen to what we want to hear, and tune out things we do not want to hear.
6. Communication is management's chief problem. The supervisor should accept the challenge to communicate more effectively and to improve interagency and intra-agency communications.
7. The supervisor may often plan for and conduct meetings. The planning phase is critical and may determine the success or the failure of a meeting.
8. Speaking before groups usually requires extra effort. Stage fright may never disappear completely, but it can be controlled.

X. SELF-DEVELOPMENT

1. Every employee is responsible for his own self-development.
2. Toastmaster and toastmistress clubs offer opportunities to improve skills in oral communications.
3. Planning for one's own self-development is of vital importance. Supervisors know their own strengths and limitations better than anyone else.
4. Many opportunities are open to aid the supervisor in his developmental efforts, including job assignments; training opportunities, both governmental and non-governmental -- to include universities and professional conferences and seminars.
5. Programmed instruction offers a means of studying at one's own rate.
6. Where difficulties may arise from a supervisor's being away from his work for training, he may participate in televised home study or correspondence courses to meet his self-develop- ment needs.

XI. TEACHING AND TRAINING

A. The Teaching Process

Teaching is encouraging and guiding the learning activities of students toward established goals. In most cases this process consists in five steps: preparation, presentation, summarization, evaluation, and application.

1. Preparation

    Preparation is twofold in nature; that of the supervisor and the employee.
    Preparation by the supervisor is absolutely essential to success. He must know what, when, where, how, and whom he will teach. Some of the factors that should be considered are:

    (1) The objectives   (5) Employee interest
    (2) The materials needed   (6) Training aids
    (3) The methods to be used   (7) Evaluation
    (4) Employee participation   (8) Summarization

Employee preparation consists in preparing the employee to receive the material. Probably the most important single factor in the preparation of the employee is arousing and maintaining his interest. He must know the objectives of the training, why he is there, how the material can be used, and its importance to him.

2. Presentation

In presentation, have a carefully designed plan and follow it.
The plan should be accurate and complete, yet flexible enough to meet situations as they arise. The method of presentation will be determined by the particular situation and objectives.

3. Summary

A summary should be made at the end of every training unit and program. In addition, there may be internal summaries depending on the nature of the material being taught. The important thing is that the trainee must always be able to understand how each part of the new material relates to the whole.

4. Application

The supervisor must arrange work so the employee will be given a chance to apply new knowledge or skills while the material is still clear in his mind and interest is high. The trainee does not really know whether he has learned the material until he has been given a chance to apply it. If the material is not applied, it loses most of its value.

5. Evaluation

The purpose of all training is to promote learning. To determine whether the training has been a success or failure, the supervisor must evaluate this learning.
In the broadest sense evaluation includes all the devices, methods, skills, and techniques used by the supervisor to keep him self and the employees informed as to their progress toward the objectives they are pursuing. The extent to which the employee has mastered the knowledge, skills, and abilities, or changed his attitudes, as determined by the program objectives, is the extent to which instruction has succeeded or failed.
Evaluation should not be confined to the end of the lesson, day, or program but should be used continuously. We shall note later the way this relates to the rest of the teaching process.

B. Teaching Methods

A teaching method is a pattern of identifiable student and instructor activity used in presenting training material.
All supervisors are faced with the problem of deciding which method should be used at a given time.
As with all methods, there are certain advantages and disadvantages to each method.

1. Lecture

The lecture is direct oral presentation of material by the supervisor. The present trend is to place less emphasis on the trainer's activity and more on that of the trainee.

2. Discussion

Teaching by discussion or conference involves using questions and other techniques to arouse interest and focus attention upon certain areas, and by doing so creating a learning situation. This can be one of the most valuable methods because it gives the employees 'an opportunity to express their ideas and pool their knowledge.

3. Demonstration

The demonstration is used to teach how something works or how to do something. It can be used to show a principle or what the results of a series of actions will be. A well-staged demonstration is particularly effective because it shows proper methods of performance in a realistic manner.

4. Performance

Performance is one of the most fundamental of all learning techniques or teaching methods. The trainee may be able to tell how a specific operation should be performed but he cannot be sure he knows how to perform the operation until he has done so.

5. Which Method to Use

Moreover, there are other methods and techniques of teaching. It is difficult to use any method without other methods entering into it. In any learning situation a combination of methods is usually more effective than anyone method alone.

Finally, evaluation must be integrated into the other aspects of the teaching-learning process.
It must be used in the motivation of the trainees; it must be used to assist in developing understanding during the training; and it must be related to employee application of the results of training.

This is distinctly the role of the supervisor.

BASIC FUNDAMENTALS OF A FINANCIAL STATEMENT

TABLE OF CONTENTS

	PAGE
Commentary	1
Financial Reports	1
Balance Sheet	1
Assets	1
The ABC Manufacturing Co., Inc.	
Consolidated Balance Sheet – December 31	2
Fixed Assets	3
Depreciation	4
Intangibles	4
Liabilities	5
Reserves	6
Capital Stock	6
Surplus	6
What Does the Balance Sheet Show?	7
Net Working Capital	7
Inventory and Inventory Turnover	8
Net Book Value of Securities	8
Proportion of Bonds, Preferred and Common Stock	9
The Income Account	10
Cost of Sales	11
The ABC Manufacturing Co., Inc.	
Consolidated Income and Earned Surplus – December 31	11
Maintenance	12
Interest Charges	13
Net Income	13
Analyzing the Income Account	14
Interest Coverage	15
Earnings Per Common Share	15
Stock Prices	16
Important Terms and Concepts	17

BASIC FUNDAMENTALS OF A FINANCIAL STATEMENT

COMMENTARY

The ability to read and understand a financial statement is a basic requirement for the accountant, auditor, account clerk, bookkeeper, bank examiner, budget examiner, and, of course, for the executive who must manage and administer departmental affairs.

FINANCIAL REPORTS

Are financial reports really as difficult as all that? Well, if you know they are not so difficult because you have worked with them before, this section will be of auxiliary help for you. However, if you find financial statements a bit murky, but realize their great importance to you, we ought to get along fine together. For "mathematics," all we'll use is fourth-grade arithmetic.

Accountants, like all other professionals, have developed a specialized vocabulary. Sometimes this is helpful and sometimes plain confusing (like their practice of calling the income account, "Statement of Profit and Loss," when it is bound to be one or the other). But there are really only a score or so technical terms that you will have to get straight in mind. After that is done, the whole foggy business will begin to clear and in no time at all you'll be able to talk as wisely as the next fellow.

BALANCE SHEET

Look at the sample balance sheet printed on Page 2, and we'll have an insight into how it is put together. This particular report is neither the simplest that could be issued, nor the most complicated. It is a good average sample of the kind of report issues by an up-to-date manufacturing company.

Note particularly that the balance sheet represents the situation as it stood on one particular day, December 31, not the record of a year's operation. This balance sheet is broken into two parts on the left are shown *ASSETS* and on the right *LIABILITIES*. Under the asset column, you will find listed the value of things the company owns or are owed to the company. Under liabilities are listed the things the company owes to others, plus reserves, surplus, and the stated value of the stockholders' interest in the company.

One frequently hears the comment, "Well, I don't see what a good balance sheet is anyway, because the assets and liabilities are always the same whether the company is successful or not."

It is true that they always balance and, by itself, a balance sheet doesn't tell much until it is analyzed. Fortunately, we can make a balance sheet tell its story without too much effort—often an extremely revealing story, particularly, if we compare the records of several years.

ASSETS

The first notation on the asset side of the balance sheet is *CURRENT ASSETS* (Item 1). In general, current assets include cash and things that can be turned into cash in a hurry, or that, in the normal course of business, will be turned into cash in the reasonably near future, usually within a year.

Item 2 on our sample sheet is *CASH*. Cash is just what you would expect—bills and silver in the till and money on deposit in the bank.

UNITED STATES GOVERNMENT SECURITIES is Item 3. The general practice is to show securities listed as current assets at cost or market value, whichever is lower. The figure, for all reasonable purposes, represents the amount by which total cash could be easily increased if the company wanted to sell these securities.

The next entry is *ACCOUNTS RECEIVABLE* (Item 4). Here we find the total amount of money owed to the company by its regular business creditors and collectable within the next year. Most of the money is owed to the company by its customers for goods that the company delivered on credit. If this were a department store instead of a manufacturer, what you owed the store on our charge account would be included here. Because some people fail to pay their bills, the company sets up a reserve for doubtful accounts, which it subtracts from all the money owed.

THE ABC MANUFACTURING COMPANY, INC.
CONSOLIDATED BALANCE SHEET – DECEMBER 31

Item			Item		
1. CURRENT ASSETS			16. CURRENT LIABILITIES		
2. Cash			17. Accts. Payable		$300,000
3. U.S. Government Securities			18. Accrued Taxes		800,000
4. Accounts Receivable (less reserves)		2,000,000	19. Accrued Wages, interest and Other Expenses		370,000
5. Inventories (at lower of cost or market)		2,000,000	20. Total Current Liabilities		$1,470,000
6. Total Current Assets		$7,000,000	21. FIRST MORTGAGE SINKING FUND BONDS, 3½ % DUE 2020		$2,000,000
7. INVESTMENT IN AFFILIATED COMPANY Not consolidated (at cost, not in excess of net assets)		200,000	22. RESERVE FOR CONTINGENCIES		200,000
8. OTHER INVESTMENTS At cost, less than market		100,000	23. CAPITAL STOCK: 24. 5% Preferred Stock (authorized and issued 10,000 shares of $100 par shares of $100 (par value)	$1,000,000	
9. PLANT IMPROVEMENT FUND		550,000			
10. PROPERTY, PLANT AND EQUIPMENT: Cost	$8,000,000		25. Common stock (authorized and issued 400,000 shares of no par value)	1,000,000	
11. Less Reserve for Depreciation	5,000,000				
12. NET PROPERTY		3,000,000			2,000,000
13. PREPAYMENTS		50,000	26. SURPLUS:		
14. DEFERRED CHARGES		100,000	27. Earned	3,530,000	
15. PATENTS AND GOODWILL		100,000	28. Capital (arising from sale of common capital stock at price in excess of stated value)	1,900,000	
					5,430,000
TOTAL		$11,000,000	TOTAL		$11,100,000

Item 5, *INVENTORIES*, is the value the company places on the supplies it owns. The inventory of a manufacturer may contain raw materials that it uses in making the things it sells, partially finished goods in process of manufacture, and, finally, completed merchandise that it is ready to sell. Several methods are used to arrive at the value placed on these various items. The most common is to value them at their cost or present market value, whichever is lower.

You can be reasonably confident, however, that the figure given is an honest and significant one for the particular industry if the report is certified by a reputable firm of public accountants.

Next on the asset side is *TOTAL CURRENT ASSETS* (Item 6). This is an extremely important figure when used in connection with other items in the report, which we will come to presently. Then we will discover how to make total current assets tell their story.

INVESTMENT IN AFFILIATED COMPANY Item 7) represents the cost to our parent company of the capital stock of its subsidiary or affiliated company. A subsidiary is simply one company that is controlled by another. Most corporations that own other companies outright lump the figures in a CONSOLIDATED BALANCE SHEET. This means that, under cash, for example, one would find a total figure that represented all of the cash of the parent company and of its wholly owned subsidiary. This is a perfectly reasonable procedure because, in the last analysis, all of the money is controlled by the same persons.

Our typical company shows that it has *OTHER INVESTMENTS* (Item 8), in addition to its affiliated company. Sometimes good marketable securities other than Government bonds are carried as current assets, but the more conservative practice is to list these other security holdings separately. If they have been bought as a permanent investment, they would always be shown by themselves. "At cost, less than market" means that our company paid $100,000 for these other investments, but they are now worth more.

Among our assets is a *PLANT IMPROVEMENT FUND* (Item 9). Of course, this item does not appear in all company balance sheets, but is typical of special funds that companies set up for one purpose or another. For example, money set aside to pay off part of the bonded debt of a company might be segregated into a special fund. The money our directors have put aside to improve the plant would often be invested in Government bonds,

FIXED ASSETS

The next item (10) is *PROPERTY, PLANT, AND EQUIPMENT*, but it might just as well be labeled Fixed Assets as these items are used more or less interchangeably, Under Item 10, the report gives the value of land, buildings, and machinery and such movable things as trucks, furniture, and hand tools. Historically, probably more sins were committed against this balance sheet item than any other.

In olden days, cattlemen used to drive their stock to market in the city. It was a common trick to stop outside of town, spread out some salt for the cattle to make them thirsty and then let them drink all the water they could hold. When they were weighed for sale, the cattlemen would collect cash for the water the stock had drunk. Business buccaneers, taking the cue from their farmer friends, would often "write up" the value of their fixed assets. In other words, they would increase the value shown on the balance sheet, making the capital stock appear to be worth a lot more than it was. *Watered stock* proved a bad investment for most stockholders. The practice has, fortunately, been stopped, though it took major financial reorganizations to squeeze the water out of some securities.

The most common practice today is to list fixed assets at cost. Often, there is no ready market for most of the things that fall under this heading, so it is not possible to give market value. A good report will tell what is included under fixed assets and how it has been valued. If the value has been increased by *write-up* or decreased by *write-down*, a footnote explanation is usually given. A *write-up* might occur, for instance, if the value of real estate increased substantially. A *write-down* might follow the invention of a new machine that put an important part of the company's equipment out of date.

DEPRECIATION

Naturally, all of the fixed property of a company will wear out in time (except, of course, non-agricultural land). In recognition of this fact, companies set up a *RESERVE FOR APPRECIATION* (Item 11). If a truck costs $4,000 and is expected to last four years, it will be depreciated at the rate of $1,000 a year.

Two other items also frequently occur in connection with depreciation—*depletion* and *obsolescence*. Companies may lump depreciation, depletion, and obsolescence under a single title, or list them separately.

Depletion is a term used primarily by mining and oil companies (or any of the so-called extractive industries). Depletion means exhaust or use up. As the oil or other natural resource is used up, a reserve is set up, to compensate for the natural wealth the company no longer owns. This reserve is set up in recognition of the fact that, as the company sells its natural product, it must get back not only the cost of extracting but also the original cost of the natural resource.

Obsolescence represents the loss in value because a piece of property has gone out of date before it wore out. Airplanes are modern examples of assets that tend to get behind the times long before the parts wear out. (Women and husbands will be familiar with the speed at which ladies' hats "obsolesce.")

In our sample balance sheet we have placed the reserve for depreciation under fixed assets and then subtracted, giving us *NET PROPERTY* (Item 12), which we add into the asset column. Sometimes, companies put the reserve for depreciation in the liability column. As you can see, the effect is just the same whether it is *subtracted* from assets or *added* to liabilities.

The manufacturer, whose balance sheet we use, rents a New York showroom and pays his rent yearly, in advance. Consequently, he has listed under assets *PREPAYMENTS* (Item 13). This is listed as an asset because he has paid for the use of the showroom, but has not yet received the benefit from its use. The use is something coming to the firm in the following year and, hence, is an asset. The dollar value of this asset will decrease by one-twelfth each month during the coming year.

DEFERRED CHARGES (Item 14) represents a type of expenditure similar to prepayment. For example, our manufacturer brought out a new product last year, spending $100,000 introducing it to the market. As the benefit from this expenditure will be returned over months or even years to come, the manufacturer did not think it reasonable to charge the full expenditure against costs during the year. He has *deferred* the charges and will write them off gradually.

INTANGIBLES

The last entry in our asset column is *PATENTS AND GOODWILL* (Item 15). If our company were a young one, set up to manufacturer some new patented product, it would probably carry its patents at a substantial figure. In fact, *intangibles* of both old and new companies are often of great but generally unmeasurable worth.

Company practice varies considerably in assigning value to intangibles. Proctor & Gamble, despite the tremendous goodwill that has been built up for *Ivory Soap*, has reduced all of its intangibles to the nominal $1. Some of the big cigarette companies, on the contrary, place a high dollar value on the goodwill their brand names enjoy. Companies that spend a good deal for research and the development of new products are more inclined than others to reflect this fact in the value assigned to patents, license agreements, etc.

LIABILITIES

The liability side of the balance sheet appears a little deceptive at first glance. Several of the entries simply don't sound like liabilities by any ordinary definition of the term.

The first term on the liability side of any balance sheet is usually *CURRENT LIABILITIES* (Item 16). This is a companion to the Current Assets item across the page and includes all debts that fall due within the next year. The relation between current assets and current liabilities is one of the most revealing things to be gotten from the balance sheet, but we will go into that quite thoroughly later on.

ACCOUNTS PAYABLE (Item 17) represents the money that the company owes to its ordinary business creditors—unpaid bills for materials, supplies, insurance, and the like. Many companies itemize the money they owe in a much more detailed fashion than we have done, but, as you will see, the totals are the most interesting thing to us.

Item 18, *ACCRUED TAXES*, is the tax bill that the company estimates it still owes for the past year. We have lumped all taxes in our balance sheet, as many companies do. However, sometimes you will find each type of tax given separately. If the detailed procedure is followed, the description of the tax is usually quite sufficient to identify the separate items.

Accounts Payable was defined as the money the company owed to its regular business creditors. The company also owes, on any given day, wages to its own employees; interest to its bondholders and to banks from which it may have borrowed money; fees to its attorneys; pensions, etc. These are all totaled under *ACCRUED WAGES, INTEREST AND OTHER EXPENSES* (Item 19).

TOTAL CURRENT LIABILITIES (Item 20) is just the sum of everything that the company owed on December 31 and which must be paid sometime in the next twelve months.

It is quite clear that all of the things discussed above are liabilities. The rest of the entries on the liability side of the balance sheet, however, do not seem at first glance to be liabilities.

Our balance sheet shows that the company, on December 31, had $2,000,000 of 3½ percent First Mortgage BONDS outstanding (Item 21). Legally, the money received by a company when it sells bonds is considered a loan to the company. Therefore, it is obvious that the company owes to the bondholders an amount equal to the face value or the *call price* of the bonds it has outstanding. The call price is a figure usually larger than the face value of the bonds at which price the company can *call* the bonds in from the bondholders and pay them off before they ordinarily fall due. The date that often occurs as part of the name of a bond is the date at which the company has promised to pay off the loan from the bondholders.

RESERVES

The next heading, *RESERVE FOR CONTINGENCIES* (Item 22) sounds more like an asset than a liability. "My reserves," you might say, "are dollars in the bank, and dollars in the bank are assets.

No one would deny that you have something there. In fact, the corporation treasurer also has his reserve for contingencies balanced by either cash or some kind of unspecified investment on the asset side of the ledger. His reason for setting up a reserve on the liability side of the balance sheet is a precaution against making his financial position seem better than it is. He decided that the company might have to pay out this money during the coming year if certain things happened. If he did not set up the "reserve," his surplus would appear larger by an amount equal to his reserve.

A very large reserve for contingencies or a sharp increase in this figure from the previous year should be examined closely by the investor. Often, in the past, companies tried to hide their true earnings by transferring funds into a contingency reserve. As a reserve looks somewhat like a true liability, stockholders were confused about the real value of their securities. When a reserve is not set up for protection against some very probable loss or expenditure, it should be considered by the investor as part of surplus.

CAPITAL STOCK

Below reserves there is a major heading, CAPITAL STOCK (Item 23). Companies may have one type of security outstanding, or they may have a dozen. All of the issues that represent shares of ownership are capital, regardless of what they are called on the balance sheet—preferred stock, preference stock, common stock, founders' shares, capital stock, or something else.

Our typical company has one issue of 5 percent PREFERRED STOCK (Item 24). It is called *preferred* because those who own it have a right to dividends and assets before the *common* stockholders—that is, the holders are in a preferred position as owners. Usually, preferred stockholders do not have a voice in company affairs unless the company fails to pay them dividends at the promised rate. Their rights to dividends are almost always *cumulative*. This simply means that all past dividends must be paid before the other stockholders can receive anything. Preferred stockholders are not creditors of the company so it cannot properly be said that the company *owes* them the value of their holdings. However, in case the company decided to go out of business, preferred stockholders would have a prior claim on anything that was left in the company treasury after all of the creditors, including the bondholders, were paid off. In practice, this right does not always mean much, but it does explain why the book value of their holdings is carried as a liability.

COMMON STOCK (Item 25) is simple enough as far as definition is concerned. It represents the rights of the ordinary owner of the company. Each company has as many owners as it has stockholders. The proportion of the company that each stockholder owns is determined by the number of shares he has. However, neither the book value of a no-par common stock, nor the par value of an issue that has a given par, can be considered as representing either the original sale price, the market value, or what would be left for the stockholders if the company were liquidated.

A profitable company will seldom be dissolved. Once things have taken such a turn that dissolution appears desirable, the stated value of the stock is generally nothing but a fiction. Even if the company is profitable as a going institution, once it ceases to function even its tangible assets drop in value because there is not usually a ready market for its inventory of raw materials and semi-finished goods, or its plant and machinery.

SURPLUS

The last major heading on the liability side of the balance sheet is SURPLUS (Item 26). The surplus, of course, is not a liability in the popular sense at all. It represents, on our balance sheet, the difference between the stated value of our common stock and the net assets behind the stock.

Two different kinds of surplus frequently appear on company balance sheets, and our company has both kinds. The first type listed is EARNED surplus (Item 27). Earned surplus is roughly similar to your own savings. To the corporation, earned surplus is that part of net income which has not been paid to stockholders as dividends. It still belongs to you, but the directors have decided that it is best for the company and the stockholders to keep it in the business. The surplus may be invested in the plant just as you might invest part of your savings in your home. It may also be in cash or securities.

In addition to the earned surplus, our company also has a CAPITAL surplus (Item 28) of $1,900.00, which the balance sheet explains arose from selling the stock at a higher cost per share than is given as its stated value. A little arithmetic shows that the stock is carried on the books at $2.50 a share while the capital surplus amounts to $4.75 a share. From this we know that the company actually received an average of $7.25 net a share for the stock when it was sold.

WHAT DOES THE BALANCE SHEET SHOW?

Before we undertake to analyze the balance sheet figures, a word on just what an investor can expect to learn is in order. A generation or more ago, before present accounting standards had gained wide acceptance, considerable imagination went into the preparation of balance sheets. This, naturally, made the public skeptical of financial reports. Today, there is no substantial ground for skepticism. The certified public accountant, the listing requirements of the national stock exchanges, and the regulations of the Securities and Exchange Commission have, for all practical purposes, removed the grounds for doubting the good faith of financial reports.

The investor, however, is still faced with the task of determining the significance of the figures. As we have already seen, a number of items are based, to a large degree, upon estimates, while others are, of necessity, somewhat arbitrary.

NET WORKING CAPITAL

There is one very important thing that we can find from the balance sheet and accept with the full confidence that we know what we are dealing with. That is net working capital, sometimes simply called working capital.

On the asset side of our balance sheet, we have added up all of the current assets and show the total as Item 6. On the liability side, Item 20 gives the total of current liabilities. *Net working capital* or *net current assets* is the difference left after subtracting current liabilities from current assets. If you consider yourself an investor rather than a speculator, you should always insist that any company in which you invest have a comfortable amount of working capital. The ability of a company to meet its obligations with ease, expand its volume as business expands and take advantage of opportunities as they present themselves, is, to an important degree, determined by its working capital.

Probably the question in your mind is: "*Just what does 'comfortable amount' of working capital mean?*" Well, there are several methods used by analysts to judge whether a particular company has a sound working capital position. The first rough test for an industrial company is to compare the working capital figure with the current liability total. Most analysts say that minimum safety requires that net working capital at least equal current liabilities. Or, put another way, current assets should be at least twice as large as current liabilities.

There are so many different kinds of companies, however, that this test requires a great deal of modification if it is to be really helpful in analyzing companies in different industries. To help you interpret the current position of a company in which you are considering investing, the *current ratio* is more helpful than the dollar total of working capital. The current ratio is current assets divided by current liabilities.

In addition to working capital and current ratio, there are two other ways of testing the adequacy of the current position. *Net quick assets* provide a rigorous and important test of a company's ability to meet its current obligations. Net quick assets are found by taking total current assets (Item 6) and subtracting the value of inventories (Item 5). A well-fixed industrial company should show a reasonable excess of quick assets over current liabilities.

Finally, many analysts say that a good industrial company should have at least as much working capital (current assets less current liabilities) as the total book value of its bonds and preferred stock. In other words, current liabilities, bonded debt, and preferred stock *altogether* should not exceed the current assets.

INVENTORY AND INVENTORY TURNOVER

In the recent past, there has been much talk of inventories. Many commentators have said that these carry a serious danger to company earnings if management allows them to increase too much. Of course, this has always been true, but present high prices have made everyone more inventory-conscious than usual.

There are several dangers in a large inventory position. In the first place, sharp drop in price may cause serious losses; also, a large inventory may indicate that the company has accumulated a big supply of unsalable merchandise. The question still remains, however: "What do we mean by large inventory?"

As you certainly realize, an inventory is large or small only in terms of the yearly turnover and the type of business. We can discover the annual turnover of our sample company by dividing inventories (Item 5) into total annual sales (item "a" on the income account).

It is also interesting to compare the value of the inventory of a company being studied with total current assets. Again, however, there is considerable variation between different types of companies, so that the relationship becomes significant only when compared with similar companies.

NET BOOK VALUE OF SECURITIES

There is one other very important thing that can be gotten from the balance sheet, and that is the net book or equity value of the company's securities. We can calculate the net book value of each of the three types of securities our company has outstanding by a little very simple arithmetic. *Book value* means *the value at which something is carried on the books of the company.*

The full rights of the bondholders come before any of the rights of the stockholders, so, to find the net book value or net tangible assets backing up the bonds we add together the balance sheet value of the bonds, preferred stock, common stock, reserve, and surplus. This gives us a total of $9,630,000, (We would not include contingency reserve if we were reasonably sure the contingency was going to arise, but, as general reserves are often equivalent to surplus, it is, usually, best to treat the reserve just as though it were surplus.) However, part of this value represents the goodwill and patents carried at $100,000, which is not a tangible item, so, to be conservative, we subtract this amount, leaving $9,530,000 as the total net book value of the bonds. This is equivalent to $4,765 for each $1,000 bond, a generous figure. To calculate the net book value of the preferred stock, we must eliminate the face value of the bonds, and then, following the same procedure, add the value of the preferred stock, common stock, reserve, and surplus, and subtract goodwill. This gives us a total net book value for the preferred stock of $7,530 or $753 for each share of $100 par value preferred. This is also very good coverage for the preferred stock, but we must examine current earnings before becoming too enthusiastic about the value of any security.

The net book value of the common stock, while an interesting figure, is not so important as the coverage on the senior securities. In case of liquidation, there is seldom much left for the common stockholders because of the normal loss in value of company assets when they are put up for sale, as mentioned before. The book value figure, however, does give us a basis for comparison with other companies. Comparisons of net book value over a period of years also show us if the company is a soundly growing one or, on the other hand, is losing ground. Earnings, however, are our important measure of common stock values, as we will see shortly.

The net book value of the common stock is found by adding the stated value of the common stock, reserves, and surplus and then subtracting patents and goodwill. This gives us a total net book value of $6,530,000. As there are 400,000 shares of common outstanding, each share has a net book value of $16.32. You must be careful not to be misled by book value figures, particularly of common stock. Profitable companies (Coca-Cola, for example) often show a very low net book value and very substantial earnings. Railroads, on the other hand, may show a high book value for their common stock but have such low or irregular earnings that the market price of the stock is much less than its apparent book value. Banks, insurance companies, and investment trusts are exceptions to what we have said about common stock net book value. As their assets are largely liquid (i.e., cash, accounts receivable, and marketable securities), the book value of their common stock sometimes indicates its value very accurately.

PROPORTION OF BONDS, PREFERRED AND COMMON STOCK

Before investing, you will want to know the proportion of each kind of security issued by the company you are considering. A high proportion of bonds reduces the attractiveness of both the preferred and common stock, while too large an amount of preferred detracts from the value of the common.

The *bond ratio* is found by dividing the face value of the bonds (Item 21), or $2,000,000, by the total value of the bonds, preferred stock, common stock, reserve, and surplus, or $9,630,000. This shows that bonds amount to about 20 percent of the total of bonds, capital, and surplus.

The *preferred stock ratio* is found in the same way, only we divide the stated value of the preferred stock by the total of the other five items. Since we have half as much preferred stock as we have bonds, the preferred ratio is roughly 10.

Naturally, the *common stock ratio* will be the difference between 100 percent and the totals of the bonds and preferred, or 70 percent in our sample company. You will want to remember that the most valuable method of determining the common stock ratio is in combination with reserve and surplus. The surplus, as we have noted, is additional backing for the common stock and usually represents either original funds paid in to the company in excess of the stated value of the common stock (capital surplus), or undistributed earnings (earned surplus).

Most investment analysts carefully examine industrial companies that have more than about a quarter of their capitalization represented by bonds, while common stock should total at least as much as all senior securities (bonds and preferred issues). When this is not the case, companies often find it difficult to raise new capital. Banks don't like to lend them money because of the already large debt, and it is sometimes difficult to sell common stock because of all the bond interest or preferred dividends that must be paid before anything is available for the common stockholder.

Railroads and public utility companies are exceptions to most of the rules of thumb that we use in discussing The ABC Manufacturing Company, Inc. Their situation is different because of the tremendous amounts of money they have invested in their fixed assets, their small inventories and he ease with which they can collect their receivables. Senior securities of railroads and utility companies frequently amount to more than half of their capitalization, Speculators often interest themselves in companies that have a high proportion of debt or preferred stock because of the *leverage factor*. A simple illustration will show why. Let us take, for example, a company with $10,000,000 of 4 percent bonds outstanding. If the company is earning $440,000 before bond interest, there will be only $40,000 left for the common stock ($10,000,000 at 4% equals $400,000). However, an increase of only 10 percent in earnings (to $484,000) will leave $84,000 for common stock dividends, or an increase of more than 100 percent. If there is only a small common issue, the increase in earnings per share would appear very impressive.

You have probably already noticed that a decline of 10 percent in earnings would not only wipe out everything available for the common stock, but result in the company being unable to cover its full interest on its bonds without dipping into surplus. This is the great danger of so-called high leverage stocks and also illustrates the fundamental weakness of companies that have a disproportionate amount of debt or preferred stock. Investors would do well to steer clear of them. Speculators, however, will continue to be fascinated by the market opportunities they offer.

THE INCOME ACCOUNT

The fundamental soundness of a company, as shown by its balance sheet, is important to investors, but of even greater interest is the record of its operation. Its financial structure shows much of its ability to weather storms and pick up speed when times are good. It is the income record, however, that shows us how a company is actually doing and gives us our best guide to the future.

The *Consolidated Income and Earned Surplus* account of our company is stated on the next page. Follow the items given there and we will find out just how our company earned its money, what it did with its earnings, and what it all means in terms of our three classes of securities. We have used a combined income and surplus account because it is the form most frequently followed by industrial companies. However, sometimes the two statements are given separately. Also, a variety of names are used to describe this same part of the financial report. Sometimes it is called profit and loss account, sometimes *record of earnings*, and, often, simply *income account*. They are all the same thing.

The details that you will find on different income statements also vary a great deal. Some companies show only eight or ten separate items, while others will give a page or more of closely spaced entries that break down each individual type of revenue or cost. We have tried to strike a balance between extremes; give the major items that are in most income statements, omitting details that are only interesting to the expert analyst.

The most important source of revenue always makes up the first item on the income statement. In our company, it is *Net Sales* (Item "a"). If it were a railroad or a utility instead of a manufacturer, this item would be called *gross revenues*. In any case, it represents the money paid into the company by its customers. Net sales are given to show that the figure represents the amount of money actually received after allowing for discounts and returned goods.

Net sales or gross revenues, you will note, is given before any kind of miscellaneous revenue that might have been received from investments, the sale of company property, tax refunds, or the like. A well-prepared income statement is always set up this way so that the stockholder can estimate the success of the company in fulfilling its major job of selling goods or service. If this were not so, you could not tell whether the company was really losing or making money on its operations, particularly over the last few years when tax rebates and other unusual things have often had great influence on final net income figures.

The ABC Manufacturing Company, Inc.
CONSOLIDATED INCOME AND EARNED SURPLUS
For the Year Ended December 31

Item			
a.	Sales		$10,000,000
b.	COST OF SALES, EXPENSES AND OTHER OPERATING CHARGES:		
c.	Cost of Goods Sold	$7,000,000	
d.	Selling, Administrative & Gen. Expenses	500,000	
e.	Depreciation	200,000	
f.	Maintenance and Repairs	400,000	
g.	Taxes (Other than Federal Inc. Taxes)	300,000	
h.	NET PROFIT FROM OPERATIONS		8,400,000
i.	OTHER INCOME:		$1,600,000
j.	Royalties and Dividends	$250,000	
k.	Interest	25,000	
l.	TOTAL		$1,875,000
m.	INTEREST CHARGES:		
n.	Interest on Funded Debt	$70,000	
o.	Other Interest	20,000	90,000
p.	NET INCOME BEFORE PROVISION FOR FED. INCOME TAXES		$1,785,000
q.	PROVISION FOR FEDERAL INCOME TAXES		678,300
r.	NET INCOME		$1,106,700
s.	DIVIDENDS		
t.	Preferred Stock - $5.00 Per Share	$50,000	
u.	Common Stock - $1.00 Per Share	400,000	
v.	PROVISION FOR CONTINGENCIES	200,000	650,000
w.	BALANCE CARRIED TO EARNED SURPLUS		456,700
x,	EARNED SURPLUS – JANUARY 1		3,073,000
y.	EARNED SURPLUS – DECEMBER 31		$3,530,000

COST OF SALES

A general heading, *Cost of Sales, Expenses, and Other Operating Charges* (Item "b") is characteristic of a manufacturing company, but a utility company or railroad would call all of these things *operating expenses*.

The most important subdivision is *Cost of Goods Sold* (Item "c"). Included under cost of goods sold are all of the expenses that go directly into the manufacture of the products the company sells—raw materials, wages, freight, power, and rent. We have lumped these expenses together, as many companies do. Sometimes, however, you will find each item listed separately. Analyzing a detailed income account is a pretty technical operation and had best be left to the expert.

We have shown separately, opposite "d," the *Selling, Administrative and General Expenses* of the past year. Unfortunately, there is little uniformity among companies in their treatment of these important non-manufacturing costs. Our figure includes the expenses of management; that is, executive salaries and clerical costs; commissions and salaries paid to salesmen; advertising expenses, and the like.

Depreciation ("e") shows us the amount that the company transferred from income during the year to the depreciation reserve that we ran across before as Item "11" on the balance sheet (Page 2). Depreciation must be charged against income unless the company is going to live on its own fat, something that no company can do for long and stay out of bankruptcy.

MAINTENANCE

Maintenance and Repairs (Item "f") represents the money spent to keep the plant in good operating order. For example, the truck that we mentioned under depreciation must be kept running day by day. The cost of new tires, recharging the battery, painting and mechanical repairs are all maintenance costs. Despite this day-to-day work on the truck, the company must still provide for the time when it wears out—hence, the reserve for depreciation.

You can readily understand from your own experience the close connection between maintenance and depreciation. If you do not take good care of your own car, you will have to buy a new one sooner than you would had you maintained it well. Corporations face the same problem with all of their equipment. If they do not do a good job of maintenance, much more will have to be set aside for depreciation to replace the abused tools and property.

Taxes are always with us. A profitable company always pays at least two types of taxes. One group of taxes are paid without regard to profits, and include real estate taxes, excise taxes, social security, and the like (Item "g"). As these payments are a direct part of the cost of doing business, they must be included before we can determine the *Net Profit From Operations* (Item "h").

Net Profit From Operations (sometimes called *gross profit*) tells us what the company made from manufacturing and selling its products. It is an interesting figure to investors because it indicates how efficiently and successfully the company operates in its primary purpose as a creator of wealth. As a glance at the income account will tell you, there are still several other items to be deducted before the stockholder can hope to get anything. You can also easily imagine that for many companies these other items may spell the difference between profit and loss. For these reasons, we use net profit from operations as an indicator of progress in manufacturing and merchandising efficiency, not as a judge of the investment quality of securities.

Miscellaneous Income not connected with the major purpose of the company is generally listed after net profit from operations. There are quite a number of ways that corporations increase their income, including interest and dividends on securities they own, fees for special services performed, royalties on patents they allow others to use, and tax refunds. Our income statement shows *Other Income* as Item "i," under which is shown income from *Royalties* and *Dividends* (Item "j"), and as a separate entry, *Interest* (Item "k") which the company received from its bond investments. The *Total* of other income (Item "l") shows us how much The ABC Manufacturing Company received from so-called *outside activities*. Corporations with diversified interests often receive tremendous amounts of other income.

INTEREST CHARGES

There is one other class of expenses that must be deducted from our income before we can determine the base on which taxes are paid, and that is *Interest Charges* (Item "m"). As our company has $2,000,000 worth of 3 ½ percent bonds outstanding, it will pay *Interest* on *Funded Debt* of $70,000 (Item "n"). During the year, the company also borrowed money from the bank, on which it, of course, paid interest, shown as *Other Interest* (Item "o").

Net Income Before Provision for Federal Income Taxes ("Item "p") is an interesting figure for historical comparison. It shows us how profitable the company was in all of its various operations. A comparison of this entry over a period of years will enable you to see how well the company had been doing as a business institution before the government stepped in for its share of net earnings. Federal taxes have varied so much in recent years that earnings before taxes are often a real help in judging business progress.

A few paragraphs back we mentioned that a profitable corporation pays two general types of taxes. We have already discussed those that are paid without reference to profits. *Provision for Federal Income Taxes* (Item "q") is ordinarily figured on the total income of the company after normal business expenses, and so appears on our income account below these charges. Bond interest, for example, as it is payment on a loan, is deducted beforehand. Preferred and common stock dividends, which are profits that go to owners of the company, come after all charges and taxes.

NET INCOME

After we have deducted all of our expenses and income taxes from total income, we get *Net Income* (Item "r"). Net income is the most interesting figure of all to the investor. Net income is the amount available to pay dividends on the preferred and common stock. From the balance sheet, we have learned a good deal about the company's stability and soundness of structure; from net profit from operations, we judge whether the company is improving in industrial efficiency. Net income tells us whether the securities of the company are likely to be a profitable investment.

The figure given for a single year is not nearly all of the store, however. As we have noted before, the historical record is usually more important than the figure for any given year. This is just as true of net income as any other item. So many things change from year to year that care must be taken not to draw hasty conclusions. During the war, Excess Profits Taxes had a tremendous effect on the earnings of many companies. In the next few years, carryback tax credits allowed some companies to show a net profit despite the fact that they had operated at a loss. Even net income can be a misleading figure unless one examines it carefully. A rough and easy way of judging how sound a figure it is would be to compare it with previous years.

The investor in stocks has a vital interest in *Dividends* (Item "s"). The first dividend that our company must pay is that on its *Preferred Stock* (Item "t"). Some companies will even pay preferred dividends out of earned surplus accumulated in the past if the net income is not large enough, but such a company is skating on thin ice unless the situation is most unusual.

The directors of our company decided to pay dividends totaling ($400,000 on the *Common Stock*, or $1 a share (Item "u"). As we have noted before, the amount of dividends paid is not determined by net income, but by a decision of the stockholders' representatives—the company's directors. Common dividends, just like preferred dividends, can be paid out of surplus if there is little or no net income. Sometimes companies do this if they have a long history of regular payments and don't want to spoil the record because of some special temporary situation that caused them to lose money. This occurs even less frequently and is more dangerous than paying preferred dividends out of surplus.

It is much more common, on the contrary, to plough earnings back into the business—a phrase you frequently see on the financial pages and in company reports. The directors of our typical company have decided to pay only $1 on the common stock, though net income would have permitted them to pay much more. They decided that the company should save the difference.

The next entry on our income account, *Provision for Contingencies* (Item "v") shows us where our reserve for contingencies arose. The treasurer of our typical company has put the provision for contingencies after dividends. However, you will discover, if you look at very many financial reports, that it is sometimes placed above net income.

All of the net income that was not paid out as dividends, or set aside for contingencies, is shown as *Balance Carried to Earned Surplus* (Item "w"). In other words, it is kept in the business. In previous years, the company had also earned more than it paid out so it had already accumulated by the beginning of the year an earned surplus of $3,073,000 (Item "x"). When we total the earned surplus accumulated during the year to that which the company had at the first of the year, we get the total earned surplus at the end of the year (Item "y"). You will notice that the total here is the same as that which we ran across on the balance sheet as Item 27.

Not all companies combine their income and surplus account. When they do not, you will find that *balance carried to surplus* will be the last item on the income account. The statement of consolidated surplus would appear as a third section of the corporation's financial report. A separate surplus account might be used if the company shifted funds for reserves to surplus during the year or made any other major changes in its method of treating the surplus account.

ANALYZING THE INCOME ACCOUNT

The income account, like the balance sheet, will tell us a lot more if we make a few detailed comparisons. The size of the totals on an income account doesn't mean much by itself. A company can have hundreds of millions of dollars in net sales and be a very bad investment. On the other hand, even a very modest profit in round figure may make a security attractive if there are only a small number of shares outstanding.

Before you select a company for investment, you will want to know something of its *margin of profit*, and how this figure has changed over the years. Finding the margin of profit is very simple. We just divide the net profit from operations (Item "h") by net sales (Item "a"). The figure we get (0.16) shows us that the company made a profit of 16 percent from operations. By itself, though, this is not very helpful. We can make it significant in two ways.

In the first place, we can compare it with the margin of profit in previous years, and, from this comparison, learn if the company excels other companies that do a similar type of business. If the margin of profit of our company is very low in comparison with other companies in the same field, it is an unhealthy sign. Naturally, if it is high, we have grounds to be optimistic.

Analysts also frequently use *operating ratio* for the same purpose. The operating ratio is the complement of the margin of profit. The margin of profit of our typical company is 16. The operating ratio is 84. You can find the operating ratio either by subtracting the margin of profit from 100 or dividing the total of operating costs ($8,400,000) by net sales ($10,000,000).

The margin of profit figure and the operating ratio, like all of those ratios we examined in connection with the balance sheet, give us general information about the company, help us judge its prospects for the future. All of these comparisons have significance for the long term as they tell us about the fundamental economic condition of the company. But you still have the right to ask: "Are the securities good investments for me now?"

Investors, as opposed to speculators, are primarily interested in two things. The first is safety for their capital and the second, regularity of income. They are also interested in the rate of return on their investment but, as you will see, the rate of return will be affected by the importance placed on safety and regularity. High income implies risk. Safety must be bought by accepting a lower return.

The safety of any security is determined primarily by the earnings of the company that are available to pay interest or dividends on the particular issues. Again, though, round dollar figures aren't of much help to us. What we want to know is the relationship between the total money available and the requirements for each of the securities issued by the company.

INTEREST COVERAGE

As the bonds of our company represent part of its debt, the first thing we want to know is how easily the company can pay the interest. From the income account we see that the company had total income of $1,875,000 (Item "1"). The interest charge on our bonds each year is $70,000 (3½ percent of $2,000,000—Item 21 on the balance sheet). Dividing total income by bond interest charges ($1,875,000 by $70,000) shows us that the company earned its bond interest 26 times over. Even after income taxes, bond interest was earned 17 times, a method of testing employed by conservative analysts. Before an industrial bond should be considered a safe investment, so our company has a wide margin of safety.

To calculate the *preferred dividend coverage* (i.e., the number of times preferred dividends were earned), we must use net income as our base, as Federal Income Taxes and all interest charges must be paid before anything is available for stockholders. As we have 10,000 shares of $100 par value of preferred stock which pays a dividend of 5 percent, the total dividend requirement for the preferred stock is $50,000 (Items 24 on the balance sheet and "t" on the income account).

EARNINGS PER COMMON SHARE

The buyer of common stocks is often more concerned with the earnings per share of his stock than he is with the dividend. It is usually earnings per share or, rather, prospective earnings per share, that influence stock market prices. Our income account does not show the earnings available for the common stock, so we must calculate it ourselves. It is net income less preferred dividends (Items "r"- "t"), or $1,056,700. From the balance sheet, we know that there are 400,000 shares outstanding, so the company earned about $2.64 per share.

All of these ratios have been calculated for a single year. It cannot be emphasized too strongly, however, that the record is more important to the investor than the report of any single year. By all the tests we have employed, both the bonds and the preferred stock of our typical company appear to be very good investments, if their market prices were not too high. The investor would want to look back, however, to determine whether the operations were reasonably typical of the company.

Bonds and preferred stocks that are very safe usually sell at pretty high prices, so the yield to the investor is small. For example, if our company has been showing about the same coverage on its preferred dividends for many years and there is good reason to believe that the future will be equally kind, the company would probably replace the old 5 percent preferred with a new issue paying a lower rate, perhaps 4 percent.

STOCK PRICES

As the common stock does not receive a guaranteed dividend, its market value is determined by a great variety of influences in addition to the present yield of the stock measured by its dividends. The stock market, by bringing together buyers and sellers from all over the world, reflects their composite judgment of the present and future value of the stock. We cannot attempt here to write a treatise on the stock market. There is one important ratio, however, that every common stock buyer considers. That is the ratio of earnings to market price.

The so-called *price-earnings ratio* is simply the earnings per share on the common stock divided into the market price. Our typical company earned $2.64 a common share in the year. If the stock were selling at $30 a share, its price-earnings ratio would be about 11.4. This is the basis figure that you would want to use in comparing the common stock of this particular company with other similar stocks.

17
IMPORTANT TERMS AND CONCEPTS

LIABILITIES
    WHAT THE COMPANY OWES—+ RESERVES + SURPLUS + STOCKHOLDERS INTEREST IN THE COMPANY

ASSETS
    WHAT THE COMPANY OWNS— + WHAT IS OWED TO THE COMPANY

FIXED ASSETS
    MACHINERY, EQUIPMENT, BUILDINGS, ETC.

EXAMPLES OF FIXED ASSETS
    DESKS, TABLES, FILING CABINETS, BUILDINGS, LAND, TIMBERLAND, CARS AND TRUCKS, LOCOMOTIVES AND FREIGHT CARS, SHIPYARDS, OIL LANDS, ORE DEPOSITS, FOUNDRIES

EXAMPLES OF:
    PREPAID EXPENSES
        PREPAID INSURANCE, PREPAID RENT, PREPAIDD ROYALTIES AND PREPAID INTEREST

    DEFERRED CHARGES
        AMORTIZATION OF BOND DISCOUNT, ORGANIZATION EXPENSE, MOVING EXPENSES, DEVELOPMENT EXPENSES

ACCOUNTS PAYABLE
    BILLS THE COMPANY OWES TO OTHERS

BONDHOLDERS ARE CREDITORS
    BOND CERTIFICATES ARE IOU'S ISSUED BY A COMPANY BACKED BY A PLEDGE

BONDHOLDERS ARE OWNERS
    A STOCK CERTIFICATE IS EVIDENCE OF THE SHAREHOLDER'S OWNERSHIP

EARNED SURPLUS
    INCOME PLOWED BACK INTO THE BUSINESS

NET SALES
    GROSS SALES MINUS DISCOUNTS AND RETURNED GOODS

NET INCOME
    = TOTAL INCOME MINUS ALL EXPENSES AND INCOME TAXES

Made in United States
North Haven, CT
03 September 2023